SELF-ESTEEM

WORKBOOK

FOR

TEENS

ANITA BOHENSKY, Ph.D

GROWTH PUBLISHING
DIVISION OF GROWTH CENTRAL, LLC
750 COLUMBUS AVENUE SUITE 9S
NEW YORK, NY 10025

SELF-ESTEEM WORKBOOK FOR TEENS

By Anita Bohensky, Ph.D.

Growth Publishing offers mental health products for individuals, parents, teachers, and mental health professionals for emotional, social, and developmental growth. For questions, comments, consultation, licenses, orders or to request a free catalogue Call Growth Publishing 1-212-749-3684

http://WholeChild.net

http://GrowthCentral.com

http://AngerHelp.com/

COPYRIGHT © 2002 ANITA BOHENSKY

-ALL RIGHTS RESERVED-

NO PART OF THIS BOOK MAY BE REPRODUCED OR TRANSMITTED IN ANY FORM OR BY ANY MEANS, ELECTRONIC OR MECHANICAL, INCLUDING PHOTOCOPYING, RECORDING, OR BY ANY INFORMATION STORAGE AND RETRIEVAL SYSTEM, WITHOUT PERMISSION IN WRITING FROM THE PUBLISHER

License to duplicate available (contact:growth@growthgroups.com)

Growth Publishing
A Division of Growth Central LLC
750 Columbus Ave. Suite 9S, New York, NY 10025

PRINTED IN THE UNITED STATES OF AMERICA

First Printing 2002

Library of Congress Cataloguing-in-Publication Data

Bohensky, Anita.
    Self-Esteem Workbook for Teens
Anita Bohensky, Ph.D.
        1st ed.
        P. cm.
        ISBN 1-893505-07-3
        1. _____ . 2. _____
        _____ . 3. Self Esteem. 4. _____ . I Title.

HM132.P44 2002   158.2
                    QB199-1699

Preface

The Self-Esteem Workbook for Teens has grown out of the Real Solution Workbook series for adults created by Richard Pfeiffer. Included in the series are Workbooks for Binge/Compulsive Eating, Anxiety/Panic, Assertiveness, Anger Management and Self-Esteem. During the time that this series has been available, many people have asked if there was a Self-Esteem Workbook especially for adolescents. It has also become clear to me that there is a growing need for this Workbook in our modern culture. The need is expressed by parents, teachers, therapists – in fact, any adults who are regularly called upon to guide and instruct adolescents – and from the teens themselves.

This Workbook would not have been possible without the ideas of my husband Richard Pfeiffer and his continued support and encouragement as I worked towards tailoring the skills and concepts for teens. I also appreciate the editing help and suggestions from my daughters, Erin and Megan Bohensky.

Finally, I want to thank the adolescents with whom I have worked over the years, as their need for help with self-esteem is what motivated my desire to create this Workbook.

A. Bohensky

Using The Workbook

For Teens

If you're planning to do this Workbook completely on your own, there are a few things you should know first. The best way to ensure that this book will work well for you is to be very honest and admit to yourself that low self-esteem has created problems for you. Because The Self-Esteem Workbook For Teens asks a great deal of you as you complete assignments, exercises and homework, and demands a lot of self-discipline, you're going to have to try to work very hard.

Some adolescents, because they are older, more mature or have a longer attention span will be able to complete more parts of this book than someone who is younger or for whom esteem problems have just not become too important so far. If you are not that interested in reading the explanations of why people have a low self-esteem, but like doing the exercises, then that's all you should do right now. Later, when you feel more ready, you can go back and complete the parts you skipped the first time around. This Workbook is meant for you to go over many times so long as you still feel out of control with your feelings. Each time you redo it, you will get more help from it.

Although The Workbook was designed to complete one session per week, you may go faster or slower, at your own pace, so that you will be able to complete the entire Workbook at least once. If at any time you feel discouraged about your ability to do the parts that you want, try talking to a parent, teacher, other adult or a friend who can give you some encouragement and help. Because The Workbook is about developing skills, and each new skill relies on what you learned in the last session, you will need to do the sessions in order, one after the other. Completion of this Workbook will pay off in many ways.

For Parents, Teachers, Therapists and other helping Adults:

How much help will your teen need with this Workbook?

Depending on their age, maturity, level of self-motivation and independence, different adolescents will require more or less active support from a parent, teacher, therapist or other helping adult. If a teen seems to want and need your active involvement, go over the first session with them. Encourage them to think about and answer whatever they can on their own. Do not suggest they answer as you would. It needs to be the teen's own input if it is to truly work for them. Look over the above section For Teens to see what has been explained to them about what parts to do and what parts they might initially want to skip.

If your adolescent seems to become motivated and "catches on" to the idea of how to work independently, allow them to work on their own. You may want to check their work after they have completed a section, as you would with homework. But allow them their own answers, not what you would have answered in their place. Help correct them only if what they have done is clearly inappropriate for the exercise.

Some teens who are younger, less highly motivated and less independent will require your active involvement for the entire length of The Workbook. Remember to give continued enthusiastic encouragement, as this is a difficult and lengthy task for any teen to complete successfully. They will need your support to do their very best.

Note for Helping Adults: Although this Workbook was designed to be completed at the pace of one session per week, it can be done more quickly or slowly depending on the needs of the particular adolescent. It does need to be completed in session order, as one skill builds on a previous one. The teen may skip the explanatory sections, if he so desires as these may be beyond the scope of his comprehension. This Workbook was designed to be reworked as the teen matures and is capable of understanding and processing a larger number of the concepts explained herein.

Note for Therapists: I have found that The Workbook can be used as a jumping off point in therapy sessions where the therapist can combine The Workbook material with issues relevant to the particular teen with whom they are working. Often using a Workbook for each adolescent in a small group can be useful.

Note about Gender Terms: The Workbook uses the pronouns *he, she, him and her* interchangeably. Often *they* or *them* are substituted for a gender pronoun. In all cases, the implication is that either a male or female could be the subject of any particular statement (unless it is obviously otherwise). The use of one pronoun or another is only for convenience and variety.

Meet Some Teens

Meet some adolescents about your age who are trying to handle their angry feelings. They will join you on your journey through this workbook. You'll get a chance to see the cause of their feelings and the helpful ways that they are learning to handle these feelings.

Hi. My name is Carlos.

Actually, I'm a pretty OK guy. I'm smart, I have cool friends and I'm no loser. But I do have a problem sometimes with my self-esteem that can get me in trouble and cause me to avoid other people and situations. I'd like to change that! So I'm going to have to find a way to feel better about myself. These are some of my friends:

Todd

Lucy

Dan

Naomi

Rosie

CONTENTS

SESSION ONE

Getting Started

Think About What You Expect to Change

The Miracle Day

Learning to Identify Your Behavior as Assertive, Aggressive, Passive, or Passive-Aggressive

Four Modes of Communicating

Learning to Distinguish Between the Four Modes

Defining Ways to Measure Change in Assertive Behavior

Self-Esteem Problems and Goals

Homework

Getting Started

You have a lot to cover in this Workbook. You're going to have some fun, but you're also going to have to work pretty hard. You can get lots of things out of this Workbook: You can learn to recognize the difference between assertive, aggressive, passive, and passive-aggressive communication, and between truths and myths about assertive behavior. You can explore your fears about being assertive. There will be homework to do, and you will begin practicing what you've learned in real situations. Most of your time will be spent learning new skills and then practicing them. There's a lot for you to do. So roll up your sleeves and let's get started.

Think About What You Expect to Change

Take a little time here at the beginning of your work to think about some of the things you're hoping to get out of this Workbook. Please try not to leave out anything, even if you think it might seem dumb or silly. If they're your ideas, they are important here.

It's natural to come to the Workbook feeling either hopeful or hopeless. Self-esteem problems develop over a long time. Your problem is not likely to disappear overnight. In a later session you will work to develop smart and sensible short-term goals that may or may not make you feel better about yourself right away, but are likely to help in the long run.

As a teen with self-esteem problems you may sometimes expect too much of yourself. This "being hard on yourself" may come up again and again as you set overly tough goals for change and growth in this Workbook. Change and growth are not about "all or nothing;" there is such a thing as *some* change and *some* growth and it is a process that takes *some* time. It is important to remind yourself of the way you have of being "hard on yourself" a lot and tell yourself that changing behavior will begin with this Workbook but continues long after it is done.

List Four Overall Goals you have for doing this Workbook:
(Such as thoughts, feelings and/or behaviors that you would like to change)*

1.

2.

3.

4.

> * An example of <u>two</u> overall goals would be: (1) Being proud of my
> accomplishments, or (2) Feeling like my teachers know and like me

---

The first exercise you will do is an "imagination" exercise. Please read all the questions and answer them as completely as you can, adding as many details as you can think of. Think of how your feelings (experiences that happen inside of you) and your actions (actual behaviors) would be different from what they are now.

When completing the question about your miracle day, it is important to include both how you will feel different and (as a result) what you would do differently or what others would see that would be different about you.

Take some time now to complete all the questions.

The Miracle Day

Exercise

1. Imagine that when you go to sleep tonight, sometime during the night while you are sleeping, a miracle happens. All the problems that brought you to The Self-Esteem Workbook For Teens are solved. When you wake up tomorrow, what would your "miracle day" be like? (Describe this miracle day with as much detail as you can).

2. Who would be the first person to notice something different about you? What would he or she notice? (Remember that people cannot see what is going on inside of you. Think about what he or she would *see* that is different in the way that you behave).

3. Who else would notice something different about you? What would these people notice?

4. If no one else would notice something different about you, what would you notice that is different about yourself?

5. Using the following scale, with 10 being your miracle day and 1 being the furthest away from your miracle day, what is the closest to your miracle day that you have ever gotten in the last year?

1   5   10

6. Describe the time in question 5 with details. Include whom you were with, what he or she noticed that was different about you, when it was and where you were, what you were doing and why you were doing it.

7. Using the same scale (10 is your miracle day, 1 is furthest away from your miracle day) where are you today?

1   5   10

Learning to Identify Your Behavior as Assertive, Aggressive, Passive, or Passive-Aggressive

Exercise

Before we talk about what assertive communication is and how it is different from other types of communication, I would like you to write down how you would usually react in each of these seven problem situations. Try to be as honest as possible, recognizing that at least some of these areas have been a problem for you. We will come back to your responses later in the session. Fill out:

1. As you walk out of a store, you realize that you have been shortchanged. You would:

    _____

    _____

    _____

    _____

2. You order a diet coke and a regular coke arrives. You would:

    _____

    _____

    _____

    _____

3. A girl (or boy) that you like very much asks to borrow your bike to go to the store. You need to be getting home right away. You would:

    _____

    _____

    _____

    _____

4. You are going to a movie with a friend who gets a phone call from a really good friend. The phone conversation goes on and on and you realize that you are going to be late if you don't leave right now. You would:

    _____

    _____

    _____

    _____

5. You've been waiting in line for a movie for 30 minutes and somebody cuts in line ahead of you. You would:

_____

_____

_____

_____

6. You are watching your favorite TV program when your older brother says, "I have to talk to you right now – it's really important". You would:

_____

_____

_____

_____

7. Your teacher criticizes you unfairly in front of your classmates. You would:

_____

_____

_____

_____

Four Modes of Communicating

Assertive Communication

Assertive Communication means clearly stating your opinion, how you feel and what you want, without violating the rights of others. The underlying idea in an assertive communication is: "You and I may have our differences, but we are equally entitled to express ourselves respectfully to one another." The major advantages of assertive communication include your involvement in making important decisions, your ability to get what you want without turning off others, the good thoughts and feelings you have when you respectfully exchange ideas with someone else, and an increase in your self-esteem.

Assertive communicators speak in a calm, clear tone of voice. They make good eye contact. They have relaxed posture. Read the following example of an assertive exchange between a teacher and a student.

Teacher: I notice you haven't handed in your report that was due on Monday and it's already Friday. I'm truly upset that you're so behind. The principal wants them all in and graded by Monday so that the better ones can be selected for the statewide competition. I'd like you to work on it over this weekend and bring it in extra early Monday morning. If you do, you'll have a much easier time next week. If you don't, we'll both be in trouble.

Todd: Yeah, I'm really behind on this project. I'm sorry, it turned out to be much more work than I realized. I'm not thrilled about having to work all weekend, but if you would please go over it with me after class, I should be able to complete it by tonight or Saturday afternoon tops. If you want, I'll drop it off to you then so you can start on the grading before Monday. I'd rather not have to be in extra early on Monday morning.

Teacher: That seems reasonable to me. Thanks.

The Reasons a Teen Communicates Assertively

- You have self respect
- You respect your personal rights
- You respect the rights of others

- You have learned that your needs are as important as those of others
- You know what your needs, thoughts, feelings, and beliefs are and that they are OK

The Results of Communicating Assertively

- You are respected by others
- You are able to have mature relationships with others
- You are successful most of the time
- Others feel valued and respected by you because you are a good model for them
- You feel in control, confident, and self respecting most of the time

Assertiveness is a skill that can be learned, not a personality trait that some are born with and others without. Nobody is always assertive. For example, you may find it easier to be assertive with strangers, but have difficulty being assertive with your parents. You may choose to be assertive with your friends in one situation and passive, aggressive, or passive-aggressive with them in another. Learning to be assertive means that you can choose when and where to assert yourself.

<u>Aggressive Communication</u>

In aggressive communication, opinions, feelings, and wants are honestly stated, but at the expense of someone else's feelings. Aggressive communicators are usually loud and direct. They tend to have excellent posture and, if possible, tower over others. Sarcasm, rhetorical questions (questions not meant to be answered), threats, negative labels, profanity, "you"-statements, absolutes such as never and nobody, finger-pointing, table pounding, hands on hips and glaring are a few of the weapons they use. Read the following example of an aggressive student speaking to a teacher:

Dan: No, I don't have my report ready and you know something? I'm not going to hand it in at all! All the choices of topics were stupid. In fact, this whole class is stupid and I don't care if I get a failing grade. I hate this class and if I have to take it over in summer school that's just fine with me. At least I won't have you for a teacher!

The Reasons a Teen May Communicate Aggressively

- You may believe that being aggressive is the only way people will respond to your needs
- You may believe that you are weak unless you bully others
- You may believe that you will not have control over others unless you act aggressively
- You may be afraid that you look weak unless you are aggressive
- You may not know how to use Self-Esteem communication

Some Reasons for Not Communicating Aggressively

- You may face retaliation (pay back) and resentment from others
- You may face loses of relationships with other people because aggressive communication brings out the same in others
- You may feel guilty and worried after you have finished communicating and have calmed down

The underlying message in aggressive communication is: "I'm superior and right and you're inferior and wrong." The advantage of aggressive behavior is that people often give aggressors what they want just to get rid of them. The major disadvantage is that aggressiveness can cause others to retaliate, try to get even in some sneaky way, or avoid dealing with the aggressor completely. Aggression tends to create uncooperative enemies with whom you have to deal in the future.

Passive Communication

In passive communication, opinions, feelings, and wants are held back altogether or expressed only partly or indirectly. The passive communicator tends to speak quietly or mumble under their breath. Eye contact is poor, and posture is often slouched yet tense, giving a message of submission. Here's an example of a passive student responding to an aggressive teacher:

Naomi: (thinking to herself) I've worked my tail off on that report. I don't have to listen to her complaints!
(out loud, after a big sigh, with a little bit of attitude) I'll get working on it, Mrs. Gross.

Why a Teen May Communicate Passively

- You mistake self-esteem for aggression or selfishness. You believe that having healthy self-esteem is being mean, hostile, or uncaring.
- You mistake passive communication for politeness. You think that to be polite you have to be passive
- You do not believe that you have Self-Esteem Rights
- You are afraid of what might happen if you behave assertively
- You expect others to consider your needs over their own (as you would do for them)

Some Reasons for Not Communicating Passively

- Others may take advantage of you or take you for granted
- You may feel angry at yourself or others (feel resentful)
- You may feel hurt and/or worried
- You may lose respect for others and/or self respect
- Others may feel pity or irritation toward you

<u>Passive-Aggressive Communication</u>

Passive-Aggressive Communication means not standing up for yourself, at first (being passive), and then later, ruining the situation. In passive-aggressive behavior, opinions, feelings, and wants are held back and not expressed honestly because the answer given to requests is "yes" but the behavior is "no". The passive-aggressive communicator tends to avoid conflict (saying "no" to another's needs). One of the problems with passive-aggressive behavior is that it does not really respect either the other person's needs (thoughts, beliefs, feelings, rights) or your own. Here's an example of a passive-aggressive teen responding to an invitation:

Rosa: Sure I'd love to come to Todd's surprise 16th birthday party on Saturday night!
(Late Saturday afternoon) I can't come to the party tonight because I have an awful stomachache.

21

Why a Teen May Communicate Passive-Aggressively

- You may believe that there is less risk of retaliation and resentment if you initially say "yes"
- You may believe that you have little power and thus cannot be direct with others
- You may lack Self-Esteem Communication skills
- You may believe in the other's rights over yours
- You may believe that Passive-Aggressive Behavior is more polite than being direct and clear

Some Reasons for Not Communicating Passive-Aggressively

- You waste time and energy by being indirect and dishonest
- Your relationships become damaged because others become resentful or disrespectful
- You may lose self respect because you get your way by being indirect and dishonest

Write down your reactions to the four modes of communicating:

_____
_____
_____
_____
_____
_____
_____
_____
_____
_____
_____
_____
_____
_____

Learning to Distinguish Between the Four Modes

Exercise

Read the following *Problem Social Scenes*. Imagine that you are teen A in the problem situation. Label your responses to the situations as assertive, aggressive, passive, or passive-aggressive. After you've completed this exercise, check the answers at the end of the session to see how well you did.

Six Problem Social Scenes

Scene 1

A. What does this look like, pre-school soccer?? You *kick* the ball when it lands in front of you – you don't just stand there looking at it!
B. I didn't have a chance to kick it and I really don't want to talk about it anymore.
A. No way am I going to ignore that play. You always try to blame everybody else when you mess up.
B. Get off my back!
A. No way! I want to take care of this problem right now.

A's behavior is___Assertive___Aggressive___Passive___Pass-Agg

Scene 2

A. Why didn't you call me last night? You know I was feeling lonely because my boyfriend is away on that trip.
B. I was too busy.
A. Too busy to call your best friend? Geez, Rosa! What's up with you?
B. Sorry, Lynn. I just forgot.
A. Forgot? Well, I think that you are not just forgetful, but thoughtless, self-centered and rude.

A's behavior is ___Assertive___Aggressive___Passive___Pass-Agg

Scene 3

A. I know this will be a big inconvenience, but would you mind changing the time of my appointment on Thursday?

B. Thursday is completely booked.

A. Well, I hate to bother you, but could you at least look at your calendar to see if there might be some other time that you could squeeze me in?

A. We're really busy here right now…call us back later.

B. All right. So sorry for the interruption.

A's behavior is ___Assertive___Aggressive___Passive___Pass-Agg

Scene 4

A. Mrs. James called and asked if we could sit for her kids this weekend so she could go to a movie with her husband. Are you free Friday night? I think it would be fun.

B. Fun? Friday night is when we're going to Jack's house for that party. I don't want to baby-sit then.

A. I'd really like to help her out and I could use some extra money. Saturday, I know you have plans, so how about Sunday?

B. Much better…I'd enjoy that.

A's behavior is ___Assertive___Aggressive___Passive___Pass-Agg

Scene 5

B. Can I borrow your car tonight, Carlos? I have to go to the library.

A. Ah…Okay. When do you need it?

B. Just from nine until ten, when it closes.

A. That means you won't need it until about quarter till nine?

B. Yea, about quarter till nine.

A. …Okay.

(About twenty till nine) Sorry, My car doesn't have enough gas in it for you to make it to the library.

A's behavior is ___Assertive___Aggressive___Passive___Pass-Agg

Scene 6
(Over lunch, A tells her friends that she doesn't believe in drinking alcohol, and they criticize her for being so childish and uncool.)

A. You certainly have the right to your opinions, but I happen to believe that drinking is dangerous because it can lead to more dangerous, out-of-control behaviors, like drunk driving or unprotected sex. I'd rather be safe than end up screwing up the rest of my life.

B. Girlfriend, you really need to loosen up and live a little. You sound like my grandmother.

A. Well, that's fine by me. She sounds like a sensible woman!

A's behavior is ___Assertive___Aggressive___Passive___Pass-Agg

Defining Ways to Measure Change in Assertive Behavior

The Purpose of the *Self-Esteem Problems and Goals* form (below) is two-fold: First, it helps you to see more clearly those social situations in which you have difficulty being assertive and to define how you would like to change your behavior. Second, at the end of the Workbook, when you re-score the form, you will be able to see the progress you've made toward achieving your goals.

Let's go through the examples as you fill out the form. On the left-hand side, under *Problem*, you briefly describe the situation in which you are having trouble being assertive. Include useful identifying information such as when, where and with whom you are having the problem. Describe the way you are behaving now.

Label it as *passive, aggressive* or *passive-aggressive*. Then, under *Goal*, state exactly how you would change your behavior.

In the third column, marked *Difficulty*, rate how hard you think it would be to be assertive in each of these situations (5 = very hard, 4 = quite hard, 3 = fairly hard, 4 = a little hard, 1 = fairly easy).

In the far right-hand column, marked *Total*, multiply the number that you gave to *Importance* by the number for *Difficulty* for each item, and then

25

add up the five numbers in this column for a total number. Write this in the bottom right-hand corner. You will come back to this and use it during the course of the Workbook. At the end of the Workbook, you will re-score the *importance* and *difficulty* of each item, and compare your original and final scores to evaluate your progress. Let's look at a few examples in the form below.

Self-Esteem Problems and Goals

Instructions: rate problems on a 1-to-5 scale based on their *importance* and the *difficulty* in achieving associated assertive behavior goals.

Five Social Situations in which I have difficulty with my assertive behavior	Importance	Difficulty	Total

Examples:

1. Problem: I always say "yes " to my friends whenever they ask me to do anything. Later, I back out with a dumb excuse (*passive-aggressive*).

   Goal: I'd like to say "no" when I don't really feel like doing what they ask.   2   x   2   =   4

2. Problem: I never ask my teacher for help (*passive*).

   Goal: I truly want to ask for help when I can't figure the problem out by myself.   1   x   3   =   3

3. Problem: I let older or bigger kids take advantage of me because I don't want to get into a fight (*passive*).

   Goal: I want to be able to tell them what I want calmly and directly without getting beaten up or embarrassed.   5   x   5   =   25

4. Problem: I get tongue-tied when I try to express something positive to my boyfriend/girlfriend, so I don't do it (*passive*).

   Goal: I want to tell him/her how much I like him/her and how much I appreciate his/her support. $4 \quad \times \quad 5 \quad = \quad 20$

5. Problem: I tend to blow up at my Mom/Dad when they don't want to do things my way (*aggressive*).

   Goal: I would like to calmly tell them what I want to do and accept having to compromise. $3 \quad \times \quad 4 \quad = \quad 12$

   Total 66

Homework: Complete the Self-Esteem Problems and Goals Form

Answers: (Six Problematic Social Scenes)
Compare your answers with the ones below:

Scene 1: *A* is aggressive. *A* uses sarcasm, rhetorical questions, "you"-messages and absolutes. He does not take into account the feelings of B, who becomes immediately resentful and uncooperative in response to accusations.
Scene 2: *A* is aggressive. The tone is accusing and blaming. *B* responds with reluctance and out of guilt.
Scene 3: *A* is passive. *A*'s timid requests, preceded by apologies, make it easy for *B* to say "no".
Scene 4: *A* is assertive. The request is specific, non-hostile, open to negotiation and successful.
Scene 5: *A* is passive-aggressive. *A* can't say "no" directly and instead initially agrees to lend his car to B. Finally, *A* later offers a lame reason for not lending the car at the last minute.
Scene 6: *A* is assertive. She calmly stands up to the opinion of the group and gives a clear, non-threatening statement of her position.

Session Two

Review of Last Session

"Feeling Bad About Yourself" (The Shame Problem)

Healthy and Unhealthy Shame

Some Things About Me

Some Things Every Teen Should Know: Survival Skills

Denial

Withdrawal

Basic Ideas Behind the Four Modes of Communication

Identifying Mistaken Ideas that People Take for Granted and Challenging them with Assertive Rights

Broken Record Technique

Role-Play

Covert Modeling

Homework

Review of Last Session

The "pink cloud" is a kind of feeling or idea that can happen for teens (and adults, too) where you start feeling really good, thinking that you're going to be getting all better without thinking about the hard work that will be needed or the setbacks that you will probably have along the way. This "pink cloud" may last for one or a few sessions. On the other hand, maybe you're having some "bad" feelings about this Workbook. It's really important to talk to someone about any "bad" feelings you are having right now and see if that will help you to keep working and start to feel better. Things will get a little rougher as you go along. It will pay off to hang in there through the rough times until you get to the end. Look over the *Self-Esteem Problems and Goals*. Be sure that your goals are definite, observable and a little bit challenging, yet possible to achieve.

"Feeling Bad About Yourself" (The Shame Problem)

Most teens can stand up to normal, temporary bad feelings about themselves. That kind of shame certainly hurts, but it will soon disappear. Good shame gives every teen (and adult, too) a message they need to hear. But for teens who live with too much shame, the bad feelings never seem to go away, no matter what you do. If a person listened to it all the time, she or he might do something terrible, or just give up in misery. This kind of shame just seems too painful to stand.

Healthy and Unhealthy Shame

Feeling shame and feeling guilt can really be confusing for anyone. So let me tell you about the difference. Guilt is when someone feels that they have *done* something wrong (like stealing some money from your parent's wallet - that would be the feeling you would get). Shame is when you feel you *are* something wrong (like you just feel badly about yourself, who you are, how you look, how you act or feel). Shame is a feeling everyone has sometimes. It can be healthy or unhealthy to feel some shame. Healthy shame is normal, lasts a short time and gives you a message that helps you to balance your thinking and behavior. Unhealthy shame lasts too long, feels too powerful and extreme, so it doesn't help make you feel balanced in your thinking and behavior. If a teen has been shamed (made to feel bad about himself) too strongly or too often, the feeling of being bad doesn't ever seem to go away. That's unhealthy shame!

Some Things About Me

Fill out the following List of Statements About Yourself. You will probably have some high numbers in some areas and low ones in others. This Self-Question Scale is meant for you to use to begin to think about and understand more about the role of shame in your life.

On a scale of 1-10 (1 being <u>not at all</u> and 10 being <u>extreme</u>) how would you rate yourself?	1	2	3	4	5	6	7	8	9	10
I worry about how I look										
When I talk about what I really think, I'm embarrassed later										
I feel self-conscious when I'm with others										
I have trouble handling criticism										
I'm afraid I'll be humiliated in front of others										
I expect others to see my flaws										
I notice my own flaws and faults daily										
When others praise me, it's hard for me to believe what they're saying										
I don't think I'm as good as other people I know										
I feel embarrassed by the way other people in my family act										
Sometimes I feel bad about myself and I don't know why										
I worry about what I'll do wrong										
I hate being evaluated, even though I know I have done a good job										
I feel embarrassed just by being near somebody who's acting dumb										

Some Things Every Teen Should Know: Survival Skills

All teenagers (and adults, too) have feelings all the time. Sometimes they're good feelings and sometimes they're pretty bad feelings. If you knew about your bad feelings all the time, it would be pretty hard to do the things you have to do every day. So people find ways to survive that help them keep those bad feelings away. Sometimes these survival skills are called "defenses." A defense is a way of not noticing the bad feelings that you are having. Sometimes a person who ignores or runs away from feelings of shame may not even see that shame is the problem at all.

Hiding from or ignoring shame may help a teen temporarily deal with feelings of pain and self-hatred, but in the long run they do not get rid of the shame. No teen can learn to use shame to feel better about him or herself by ignoring it. Defenses against shame are survival skills only; teens that feel really bad about themselves can never learn that they are valuable and good people who are worth love and respect simply by pushing those feelings out of awareness.

Now we will talk about the first two defenses against shame.

Denial

The first kind of defense is called *denial*.

A teen who is in denial just doesn't know that she is feeling shame deep down inside. She fools herself into believing that she feels good about who she is when she would be feeling great shame if she was really aware of what was going on inside. She badly wants to believe that she is completely acceptable to herself and others, and so blinds herself to whatever would bring her shame.

A teen who is badly shamed often lives in a world of appearances (how you look to others). He will do anything to protect his image as the cool or popular guy, even if that means ignoring how things really are. For example, many teenagers and adults who live in a family where the parents are constantly fighting or are divorced deny that the fighting or the divorce is a problem for them. They would feel terrible shame if they admitted that their parents could not get along or no longer wanted to be together. They believe something is very wrong with the whole family of anyone who is powerless to control their feelings or behavior. They cannot understand how someone could be constantly angry or have decided to split up their family, and be a good person at the same time. As children of those people, they also must be of no value. So they tell themselves that there is really no problem.

Denial of shame is not only about unhappy marriages or divorce. Many less obvious or serious things about who you or your family are can make a teen feel bad about himself; in other words, feel ashamed. Whatever brings shame to someone can be hidden from him or her by denial. But the problem is, denial can really get to you. Feelings of worthlessness and not being able to control your feelings can sneak through. It's so important, when you really want to get over your self-esteem problems, to face up to the truth of what is, even though it hurts a lot. But you can only do that when you learn that you can stand up to your shame and survive. The only way out of shame is to come out of hiding!

Withdrawal

 Another survival skill against shame is *withdrawal* (running away). Adolescents withdraw when they have been hurt by shame, and being around other people is too hard to handle. Running away is a normal reaction at times when a teen feels open to attack and easily hurt. Withdrawal is a common reaction to shame. Remember that the first reaction of your body to shame is to look down or to the side. It's like saying to another teen, parent or teacher: "Right now I feel so bad about myself that I can't even look you in the eye. I can't feel close to you because that will only make me feel more shame." A teen who is feeling very bad about who he is, at least temporarily, believes that everyone can see right inside him, and see that he is bad and won't be good at anything he does. Teens who are feeling very ashamed withdraw in other ways, too. They avoid talking about things about which they feel stupid; they stay away from being friendly or close to other kids. Some teens like this try to stay invisible. They are always around, but never seen. Or, sometimes, they use substances (such as alcohol or drugs) to make themselves feel less involved with others. Can you think of any teen or adult that you know who uses withdrawal as a defense? Is there a part of you that can use this defense? How did you learn it?

Basic Ideas Behind the Four Modes of Communication

Assertive communication is based on the idea that adult individuals are the best judges of their own thoughts, feelings, wants and behavior. They are better informed than anyone else about their heredity, history and the current circumstances that shape them into unique human beings. Adolescents, as adults-in-training, are moving in this direction. And, as long as they are not likely to endanger themselves or others, teens should, in many situations, be allowed the same rights as the adult. Exceptions to this rule are situations where adult authority figures are responsible for a teen's behavior (such as when the teen is at home, in school or learning to play a sport). Even in those situations, you, the teen, have the right to be treated with respect and kindness. Rather than overpower the meek or give in to the aggressors, you have the right to choose to express your position and try to negotiate differences.

Passive people tend to believe that their feelings, beliefs, and opinions are not as important or valid as those of other people. As children, they learned to seek validation and guidance from their elders, and to doubt their own perceptions and judgment. As teens, they tend to give in to or are easily led by others. When they encounter a conflict between what they truly want to do and what someone else expects of them, they tend to feel guilty, wrong, anxious, stupid or put-down; and they often end up giving in to the other person.

Teenagers who often use the aggressive mode of communication seem to have an inflated sense of their own importance and feel entitled to getting whatever they want without considering the rights or sensitivities of others. Often buried under this layer of self-importance is a damaged self. As children, aggressive teens were often dominated or abused by their elders, and later took on the aggressive mode of behavior instead of being a passive victim. Other aggressive teens learned to believe from early childhood experiences that they are superior, and therefore, entitled to dominate others. Prejudice learned in childhood can lead to subtle, as well as open, aggression in teens and adults. People who are aggressive need to learn to consider the rights and feelings of others, as well as their own.

Adolescents who tend toward passive-aggressive communication sometimes believe that it will be too uncomfortable to be direct about their feelings, beliefs, and opinions. So they agree or say 'yes' to requests or demands of them. As children, they often received messages that it was not okay for them to say 'no' or express something different from others. Being different was not acceptable to mom or dad and as a result caused great conflict or was simply not allowed. So the child learned how to say 'yes' initially and to later ruin the situation.

Identifying Mistaken Ideas that People Take for Granted and Challenging them with Self-Esteem Rights

While children have no choice about ideas people take for granted and then teach their children, adults (and teens, who are learning to be adults) have to decide whether or not they are going to hold on to beliefs that discourage self-esteem and create stressful feelings. Each of the following mistaken beliefs violates a legitimate (that is, acceptable and logical) adult right. As you read each of these, put a check mark by any of the mistaken ideas that you still believe in and the legitimate rights you have difficulty accepting.

Ideas People Take for Granted	*Your Self-Esteem Rights*	
1. It's selfish to put your needs before others.	You have a right to put yourself first sometimes.	
2. It's shameful to make mistakes.	You have a right to make mistakes.	
3. If you can't convince someone your feelings are reasonable, then they must be wrong.	You have a right to be the final judge of your feelings and accept them as legitimate.	
4. You should accept the views of others, especially if they are in a position of authority. Keep your opinions to yourself.	You have a right to express your own opinions and beliefs.	
5. You should always try to be logical and consistent.	You have a right to change your mind.	
6. You should be flexible and adjust. Others have good reasons for their actions and it is impolite to question them.	You have a right to question what you don't like and protest unfair treatment.	
7. You should never interrupt or ask for clarification. Asking questions shows your stupidity.	You have a right to interrupt people.	
8. Things could even get worse; don't rock the boat.	You have a right to negotiate for change.	

35

9. You shouldn't take up others' valuable time with your emotional problems.		You have a right to ask for help or support.
10. People don't want to hear that you feel bad, so keep it to yourself.		You have a right to feel and express pain.
11. When someone takes time to give you advice, you should take it seriously.		You have a right to ignore advice of others.
12. Knowing that you have something special or have done something well is its own reward. People don't like showoffs. Success is secretly disliked and envied. Be modest when complimented.		You have a right to receive recognition for your special qualities and talents and for your work and achievements.
13. You should always try to accommodate others. If you don't, they won't be there when you need them.		You have a right to say "no" to other people's requests.
14. Don't be antisocial. People will think that you don't like them if you say that you would rather be alone than with them.		You have a right to be alone, even if others request your company.
15. You should always give other people a good reason for what you feel or do.		You have a right not to justify yourself to others.
16. When someone is in trouble, you should give help.		You have a right to decide whether you want to help.
17. You should be sensitive to the needs and wishes of others, even when they are unable to tell you what they want.		You have a right not to anticipate the needs and wishes of others.
18. It's always a good policy to stay on people's good sides.		You have a right not to worry about the goodwill of others.
19. It's not nice to put people off. If questioned, give an answer.		You have a right to choose not to respond to a question or situation.
20. You should be able to answer all questions about a field of knowledge with which you are familiar.		You have a right to say "I don't know" or "I don't understand."

"It is shameful to make mistakes". How many times, as a child, did you hear, "shame on you!" when you made a mistake? The unspoken message was that if you did something incorrectly, it was bad, and you were bad for doing it. Your value as a person depended on your actions, so it became very important to do well and please others in order to feel good as a person. When self-worth becomes closely tied to performance, then shame is what you feel when you make a mistake. You would only feel regret if you saw your mistake as an error in performance. Regret is a useful emotion because it motivates you to correct your mistakes (and try harder) the next time. Shame can serve the same function, but it also wears away at your self-esteem and contributes to compulsive over-achieving. Teens who are prone to shame believe that only 100 percent is good enough.

If you believe that it's shameful to make a mistake, you are likely to avoid taking risks, even if it means giving up your rights. Other people will use your fear and shame about making mistakes to take advantage of you. For example, when you ask for a raise (or mention that you would like a raise), your boss responds with "I seem to remember that you forgot to call in when you were sick earlier this year. That's not the behavior of someone who deserves a raise." Or you ask your coach if you can play more often during games and he reminds you of the time you struck out. In either situation, you back down because you agree with them. The association of mistakes with shame stops your assertive behavior.

Now, think about your assertive right to make mistakes. Just as a toddler learns to walk by falling down many times, you learn from your mistakes. Something worth doing right is worth doing wrong first. Mistakes have the added benefit of keeping you humble (not being too full of yourself). No one is perfect. It is human to err (make errors). This assertive right does not free you from the consequences of your errors; you are still responsible for your actions. But it frees you from the shame of equating your actions with your self-worth. A healthy dose of regret is a good enough incentive for you to minimize and correct your errors; you do not need shame, too.

When you can simply acknowledge your mistakes and not feel ashamed of them, you become harder to manipulate. For instance, when your boss points out that you failed to call in sick earlier this year, and uses this as the reason for not giving you a raise, you don't have to give up in shame. You answer with, "You're right, I did make that one mistake for which I'm sorry. Now let's talk about the things I've done right on the job." And when your coach mentions your mistaken plays as an excuse for not playing you more often during games, you don't have to feel shame, you just mention the good plays you've made and encourage him to give you a chance. Belief in the freedom to make mistakes allows you to learn, take risks and be spontaneous and creative. It supports your assertive behavior.

You may still be convinced that some of your "Mistaken Ideas that People Take for Granted" above are really correct, or you may be having a hard time accepting one of your "assertive rights." While some of these ideas may have been true for you as a child, ask yourself if they are still just as true for you as an adolescent and whether they could possibly remain true for you when you become an adult. As a teen (and even more so as an adult), do and will you have alternate ways of coping with the conditions of your life? How would these "ideas that people take for granted" get in the way of your assertive behavior?

Exercise

List on a separate piece of paper the *Mistaken Ideas That People take for Granted* which you still believe and *Self-Esteem Rights* you still question. Make a note next to each idea listed, and how you came to believe it. Think carefully about whether the conditions in which you learned it are still true for you today (and whether you expect them to remain true, as you grow to adulthood). If not, do you really want to continue to behave as though they were? For example, if you were smacked, yelled at or given disapproving looks for interrupting and questioning adults, would that really happen to you now (or in years to come)? If the answer is "yes," do you have any options open to you now that you didn't when you were younger? How does your *mistaken idea* get in the way of your self-esteem?

Continue to explore the origin of your particular *mistaken beliefs*, as well as thinking about how your *assertive rights* support self-esteem and your *mistaken ideas* do not. This is usually best done in writing. Repeat daily your *assertive rights*, and behave as though you believe them. Post your *assertive rights* in a place where you can read them often as an external reminder. With enough practice, you will eventually internalize the knowledge of your *self-esteem rights* at more than the intellectual level.

Broken Record Technique

The good news is that you have the right to express what you think, feel, and want. The bad news is that most people in the world have not participated in The Self-Esteem Workbook for Teens Program. Many will try to ignore or destroy your efforts to stand up for your rights. The *Broken Record Technique* is one of *seven* self-esteem skills that will help you deal more effectively with uncooperative and manipulative people (adults and other teens).

When a record is broken, it repeats the same piece of music over and over again. The key to *the Broken Record Technique* is persistent repetition in the face of difficulty. You will need to remember your legitimate rights if you are not to be manipulated into giving in to individuals whose interests are different than your own. Occasionally you meet people – sales people, children or a stubborn friend – who will not take "no" for an answer. When you want to set limits and someone else is having difficulty getting your message, you need to take a stand and stick to it.

This approach is also effective in telling people what you want, when their own wishes are preventing them from seeing yours. Examples include when a friend wants to copy your homework to use for her class; when you want to go home and your boss wants you to work overtime for the fifth weekend in a row; when you want to return a defective item and get your money back from a sales clerk; when your boyfriend wants to touch you in an uncomfortable way; or when your peers want to involve you in an inappropriate activity.

Here are the *five steps* of the *Broken Record Technique*:

1. Decide exactly what you want or don't want. Review your thoughts about the situation, your feelings, and your rights.

2. Create a brief, specific, easy-to-understand statement about what you want. One sentence is best. Give no excuses or explanations. Do not say "I can't." The other person will point out to you that this is just another excuse and show you how you "can." It's much simpler and more truthful to say "I don't want to." Eliminate any loopholes in your brief statement that the other person could use to back up his or her position.

3. Use body language to support your statement: good posture, direct eye contact, and a calm, confident and determined voice.

4. Firmly repeat your brief statement, as many times as necessary for the person to get your message and to realize that you won't change your mind. He or she will probably invent a number of excuses or simply say "no." Eventually, even the most aggressive person will run out of "nos" and excuses, if you are persistent. Change your brief statement only if the other person finds a serious loophole in it.

5. You may want to acknowledge the other person's opinions, feelings or wants before returning to your broken record (for example: " I know you say that all your past girl friends went all the way with you, but I'm different. I have to do what feels right for me."). Do not feel obligated to answer questions. Be careful not to be distracted from your goal.

Role-Play

A very helpful technique that can be used to reinforce your new skills is called *role-play*. Here you practice actually using assertive communication in one of your problem social situations, with another person. Ideally, you will become aware of other teens that are also working on self-esteem problems and will welcome the opportunity to *role-play* with you. Or there is a parent, therapist, teacher, or other helping adult who can *role-play*, too. But, if you are working on this problem completely on your own, this may be your opportunity to assertively communicate to a friend or supportive adult that you would like their help in this activity. Most people really enjoy *role-playing*, once they get into the swing of it.

Example of Role-Play

Step 1

Lucy: (thinking to herself): I've baby sat four weekends in a row for Mrs. Lane. I'm really sick and tired of all work and no play. I really don't want to work this weekend, but I'm afraid of what she'll say if I tell her I won't do it. I know I have the right to decide if I don't want to work and put my own needs first for a change.

Step 2

Lucy: (thinking to herself): Let's see, what excuse could I give her? I could say my mother's sick and I have to stay home and help, but she could call and check that out. I'll just tell her I don't want to baby sit tonight and not give any dumb excuse that she can get around.

Step 3 and 4

Mrs. Lane: I hate to ask you to baby sit again this weekend, but I don't have anyone else and we have to go to Mr. Lane's 40th birthday celebration.

Lucy: I know that's an important gathering, but I really can't help you out this weekend.

Mrs. Lane: I didn't think you were the kind of person to let me down at a time like this. I really need your help.

Lucy: I understand you're very disappointed that I can't help you this weekend, but I'm not going to be able to sit for you.

Mrs. Lane: But if you don't sit for me, what will we do?

Rosa: I know you need someone to sit if you want to go out and I'd be happy to give you the names of a few friends who might be able to help, but I'm not going to be able to do it.

Mrs. Lane: Well, I can't force you to sit for me…but I certainly would be interested to see how this gets worked out.

Lucy: Me too.

Exercise

Write down three situations in your life for which a *Broken Record Technique* would be suitable. For example, you might write down: "I want to return the CD to the store where I bought it and get my money back." "I want to tell my older sister not to come in and change the channel when I'm watching a program on TV." "I want to tell my friend to pay me back the $10 he borrowed from me a month ago."

Covert Modeling

This is a strategy for changing behavior from less useful to more useful and positive. The techniques of change are the behaviors suggested in the Workbook (such as *The Broken Record Technique*). The "models" for these behaviors are actually your <u>imagining</u> yourself performing these new, more positive behaviors and the reactions of others with whom you interact.

Example of Covert Modeling

Start with the easiest situation, and go through the first two steps of the *Broken Record Technique*. Write down your broken record statement. For instance, you might write, "I'm returning this CD that I bought here last weekend and I want my money back." You may choose to acknowledge what the other person said or briefly clarify a point, but don't let yourself be distracted from your statement.

Close your eyes and relax. As in the example you just went through, imagine using your broken record statement in a dialogue in which you also go over how the other person might respond. If you can't imagine yourself successfully using the broken record statement in a dialogue, imagine someone else doing it. You may want to write down the dialogue later as a script. Repeat this process for another two situations in your life for which the *Broken Record Technique* would be appropriate.

Homework

Practice successfully using the *Broken Record Technique* in situations from your own life. Other ways to practice at home include writing out the dialogue in script form, *role-playing* the dialogue in front of a mirror, with a friend or supportive adult, or recording it on tape. Finally, use the *Broken Record Technique* in real life. After your experiment, ask yourself what worked and what needed improvement. Remember to give yourself credit for practicing a new behavior, no matter what the outcome. That's always a very hard thing to do!

Note: Keep a written record of your assignments, including instructions and a brief description of what you actually do and when. Include any bright ideas or questions that come up for you. This will increase the likelihood of successfully completing your homework.

SESSION THREE

How Teens Survive Shame (The Shame Problem, continued)

Perfectionism

Rage

Review Homework

Confronting Your Fears About Being Assertive

Self-Esteem Rights

Philosophy of Self-Esteem Rights

Responsibilities of Self-Esteem Rights

Conflict of Self-Esteem Rights

Self-Esteem Log

Homework

How Teens Survive Shame (The Shame Problem, continued)

 *A two-year-old child explores the world. He finds a special place in the garden where he digs happily in the soft soil. He feels proud of himself and what he can do. "Look at me,' he wants to tell the world. "Look at what I can do. I am good."*

"Just look at you!" shouts his mother. "Look at this mess. You're dirty. Your clothes are ruined. I'm very disappointed with you. You should be ashamed of yourself."

The child feels very small. He drops his head and stares at the ground. He sees his dirty hands and clothes and begins to feel dirty inside. He thinks there must be something very bad about him, something so bad he will never really be clean. He hears his mother's disappointment. He feels bad about who he is.

Shame is not the feeling that you have *done* something wrong. Shame is the feeling that you *are* something wrong. The little boy in the story above took inside the judgment of his mother. The mother's words came just at the stage of growth when a child is beginning to feel and act a little bit independent. Two years old is the age when children first begin to become their own special self, to say "No: I'm not you...I'm me." If his mother has a problem with her child being independent from her, the child is probably going to feel a lot of shame.

These are some thoughts a very shamed teen could feel:

- I am damaged (broken, a mistake)

- I am dirty (soiled, ugly, unclean, filthy, disgusting)

- I am not able (not good enough, not smart enough)

- I am useless (worthless)

- I am unwanted (unloved, unappreciated)

- I deserve to be abandoned (forgotten, left out, rejected)

- I am weak (helpless, dependent, defenseless)

- I am bad (awful, dreadful, evil)

- I am nothing (invisible, unnoticed, empty)

● I am a freak (not like other people, strange, weird, creepy)

Remember: Defenses against these bad feelings help a teen deal with their self-worth problems temporarily, but in the long run, they do not erase the shame. No teen can learn to benefit from shame by ignoring it. Defenses against shame are for survival only; very shamed teens must learn and experience that they are valuable people who are worthy of love and respect.

Perfectionism

Another way to hide from or ignore shame is called *perfectionism*. A perfectionist hates making mistakes because he thinks mistakes prove that something is very wrong with him as a person. If he fails at just one thing he believes that he is a total failure.

The teen who is a perfectionist and defending against his bad and shameful feelings seems to believe only in two different states: perfect or shameful (all or nothing). This kind of teen fights hard against being human because he sees his humanity as a type of failure. He can't believe that all people are only human and have to make do with whatever their abilities allow them. It is not shameful for anyone, adult or child, to be less than perfect when none of us has a choice in the matter.

A perfectionist needs to excel at something, and will often go to extremes to prove himself. Perhaps he stays up late into the night obsessing over a simple homework assignment that should only have taken a half-hour. Or she spends hours everyday on the tennis court, practicing her backhand until it is just right, and ignoring her coach's advice to rest her painfully sore elbow, or he works out at the gym or runs for hours a day.

As you can see, the perfectionist is in a no-win situation. No matter how smart, how strong or brave, or how well she performs, despite all her successes, she never feels more than one step ahead of her shame. She is constantly feeling that other teens and adults are watching and noticing any mistake she could make and will then judge her as worthless. Perhaps by working harder or longer than anyone else she will be able to delay her bad feelings for just a little while longer. But she cannot feel comfortable for very long because she does not know how to accept herself as a good, but limited, human being.

Can you think of anyone (adult or teen) who uses perfectionism as a defense? Is there a part of you that can use this defense? How did you learn it?

Rage

What happens when a teen who feels terribly badly about himself and deeply shamed cannot withdraw from a threatening situation? *Rage*, another likely way to survive shame, is a common response. The "rageful" adolescent seems like he's shouting a warning: "Don't get any closer! You are getting too close to seeing my shame, and I won't let anyone see that part of me. Stay away or I will attack." A rageful teen is desperate to keep others far enough away so that they cannot destroy him.

Teens are most likely to fly into a rage when they are surprised by a sudden attack that threatens their identity – their idea of who they are. For example, a friend might tell his buddy that he dresses like a nerd, and isn't cool enough to be accepted by the popular kids. The friend might just be joking, not trying to hurt his buddy. But his buddy reacts in rage: "What do you mean? I look a whole lot cooler than you do - at least I'm not a fat porker like you." This shamed teen can only think to defend him or herself by cruelly attacking the other kid, even if that person is a friend.

Rage works. It drives other people away and in doing so, protects the teen from allowing others to see the parts of himself of which he is ashamed. Sometimes it works too well. People start to avoid angry and rageful teens who are overly sensitive to what they feel are insults. "I would like to be Stephanie's friend", a girl might say, "but whenever we start to get friendly, she always finds something to get mad about. Then she's mean to me for no reason."

The rageful teen's way of defending himself against the terribly strong feeling that he is no good (filled with shame) is very hard on his self-esteem. This teen will probably feel even worse about himself when others become too scared or angry to reach out to him. Very angry teens become trapped in a lonely world of their own making. Any teen might get angry once in awhile, especially when they are suddenly and unexpectedly embarrassed or shamed. But teens who live with a lot of shame may express their anger more often. Their regular reactions of rage cover up deep feelings of worthlessness and shame. Their attacks on others take attention away from their own bad feelings.

Can you think of anyone who uses rage as a defense? Is there a part of you that can use this defense? How did you learn it?

Review Homework

Review the five steps of the *Broken Record Technique.* What did you do since the last session with the technique?

Confronting Your Fears About Being Assertive

1. If I use assertive behavior in this situation with so-and-so (a friend, parent or teacher), what is the worst thing that can happen?

2. What beliefs do I have that would make this more likely to happen?

3. Is there evidence to support this belief?

4. What evidence do I have that goes against this belief?

5. What would be a more realistic negative outcome of my being assertive in this situation?

6. How might I respond to or cope with this more realistic outcome?

7. What is the best thing that could happen?

8. What is going to happen if I continue to do what I have been doing?

9. Is it worth it to me to be assertive in this situation? (Consider your responses to questions 5 – 8 before answering.)

Answer the questions to "Confronting My Fears About Being Assertive" using the following examples as help:

1. If I use assertive behavior in this situation with so-and-so, what is the worst thing that could happen? (Example: If I ask Dan to help me with soccer practice and he says "no," will I feel worthless?)

2. What beliefs do I have that would make this more likely to happen? (Example: I'd have to believe that my self-worth is dependent on Dan agreeing to help me.)

3. Is there any evidence to support this belief? (Example: Not really.)

4. What evidence is there that goes against this belief? (Example: My self-worth is independent of Dan's opinion of me. I value myself as a person; I have a lot of good qualities and I am a good friend, athlete and musician.)

5. What would be a more realistic negative outcome of my being assertive in this situation? (Example: Dan could say "no," probably for a good reason, in which case I would be disappointed).

6. How might I respond to or cope with this negative outcome? (Example: I would feel disappointed for a short while, but I would remind myself of my value as a person and that one rejection, on one occasion, doesn't destroy my worth. I would talk to my best friend about it, and then I would ask someone else to help me with soccer practice.)

7. What is the best thing that could happen? (Example: Dan could say "yes" and we could get to know each other better at the same time.)

8. What is going to happen if I continue to do what I am doing? (Example: I will have to practice soccer on my own. Or get someone else to help me.

9. Is it worth it to me to be assertive in this situation? (Weigh your responses to questions 5 – 8 before answering.) (Example: It is worth the risk of being disappointed by Dan saying "no," on the chance that I

will get his help instead of playing alone or finding someone else to help me.)

Exercise

Go over your answers to the questions above as you review the *Mistaken Ideas that People take for Granted* and *Self-Esteem Rights* from Session Two. What did you notice?

Self-Esteem Rights

Self-Esteem Rights are so important for teens to recognize and understand, that some time will be spent reviewing and learning about them in detail.

1   You have a right to put yourself first sometimes

2   You have a right to make mistakes

3   You a right to be the final judge of your feelings and accept them as legitimate

4   You have a right to express your own opinions and beliefs

5   You have a right to change your mind

6   You have a right to question what you don't like and to protest unfair treatment

7   You have a right to interrupt or to ask for clarification

8   You have a right to negotiate for change

9   You have a right to ask for help or emotional support

10 You have a right to feel and express pain or uncomfortable feelings

11 You have a right to ignore advice of others

12   You have a right to receive recognition for your special qualities and talents and for your work and achievements

13   You have a right to say "no" to other people's requests

14   You have a right to be alone, even if others request your company

15   You have a right not to justify yourself to others

16   You have a right not to take responsibility for somebody else's problem

17   You have a right not to have to anticipate the needs and wishes of others

18   You have a right not to worry about the good will of others

19   You have a right to choose not to respond to a question or situation

20   You have a right to say "I don't know" or "I don't understand"

Philosophy of Self-Esteem Rights

Many times adolescents are not sure about how they would like to behave in a particular situation because they are unclear about what *rights* they have and what *rights* belong to others. Rights are the expression of a person's values. They are the beliefs that allow us to lead our lives the way we want. They are something we must claim on our own, even though others(such as parents, teachers and clergy) try to teach us theirs.

We may believe that others have rights, but we do not accept them for ourselves. For example, we may think others have the right to say "no" to someone's request (i.e. "Can you help me study for the test on Saturday?") but that we do not have the same right. The philosophy of self-esteem rights is based on the belief that all persons are created equal on a human level and all deserve the fundamental right to express their thoughts, needs, and feelings.

Responsibilities of Self-Esteem Rights

Having self-esteem rights does not mean having license to do whatever you want. You must always remember that the other person also has the right to express their needs, make mistakes, and so on. There are responsibilities with each right. For example, the responsibilities that are attached to the right to make a mistake include acknowledging the fact that a mistake was made, not making the same mistake over and over again, and accepting other people's right to make mistakes.

Conflict of Self-Esteem Rights

Frequently a situation between two people (such as two teens, or an adult and a teen) will involve a conflict between each person's rights. When this occurs, it is important to take a flexible rather than a rigid stance. Can a creative compromise be worked out? Life is often unfair. We can expect to be treated with respect, but we can also expect that others will sometimes treat us unfairly. It is often best not to take unfair treatment personally or to dwell upon the injustice of how you have been treated. Self-esteem can be increased by simply expressing your opinion i.e. "It is not fair that …."

The Self-Esteem Behavior Log

The Self-Esteem Behavior Log is an indispensable tool for self-observation, supporting change, and watching your progress. Use the *Self-Esteem Behavior Log* on the following page to record *Self-Esteem Behavior* situations each week. You can make copies of the Log on the next page or the one found in the Appendix.

Fill out the Log using the following criteria:

Date - Record the date of the situation.

Behavior – Record and describe your self-esteem behavior. *For example: Refused a request.*

Person – Whom did you interact with? *For example: My classmate.*

+ Aspects – Describe the positive aspects of your self-esteem behavior. *For example: Good eye contact ("I looked right at him").*

- Aspects – Describe the negative aspects of your self-esteem behavior. *For example: sarcasm("I had a wise-guy attitude").*

Aggressive, Passive, Passive-Aggressive, or Assertive - Describe your behavior as either aggressive, passive, passive-aggressive, or assertive – *as you look back at the definitions for each type of self-esteem behavior described in Session One.*

Self Esteem Behavior Log

Date	Behavior	Person	+ Aspects	- Aspects	Aggressive, Passive, Passive-Agg, Assertive

Homework: Self-Esteem Behavior Log

Keep the log during the next week. You will need to make copies. Anticipate problems with completing the assignment and know that you don't have to do it perfectly; even doing it some of the time will be helpful. Review the *Self-Esteem Rights* in the Appendix.

For each of your five specific assertiveness problems and goals, answer the nine questions under **Confronting Your Fears About Being Assertive.** Continue practicing the *Broken Record Technique.* Remember to keep a written record of your homework experiences.

Session Four

The Shame Problem (continued)

Constant Shame Feels Terrible

Arrogance

Exhibitionism

Review Homework

Criticism as a Form of Manipulation

Acknowledgement

Clouding

Three Ways to Diffuse Manipulative Criticism

Agree in Part

Agree in Probability

Agree in Principle

Homework

The Shame Problem (continued)

Constant Shame Feels Terrible

A young adolescent has almost no idea of who he is or wants to be. He tries to please everyone he meets, to become whatever they want him to be. He wears a mask of niceness so well that even he has no idea of what would happen if he took it off. He thinks that if people were to see through his mask, they would discover that he is worthless or disgusting. They might never want to speak to him again.

Constantly feeling bad about who you are is a terrible feeling. Getting over this feeling means you have to give up the imaginary idea that you have to live with constant shame. We call this situation an "imaginary idea" because nobody really has to live forever in shame. There is room enough for everybody in this world. There is no such thing as a "subhuman." The wonderful thing about shame, even terrible, constant shame, is that teens (and adults, too) can learn to live with it and grow healthier and happier with it. But the person who is deeply shamed must learn to question his or her belief that deep down inside, he or she has no value or worth. Shamed teens become used to seeing everything that happens to them as proof that they are no good or not good enough. They need to start questioning and eventually, throw away their own make-believe idea that they have to go through life feeling bad about who they are. For example, the boy described above will need to begin to accept his own good qualities and find the courage to take off his mask so that he can discover his true self.

In this section you will learn how to:

- Stop Putting Yourself Down

- Stop Comparing Yourself To Other Teens and Adults

- Change Relationships That Make You Feel Ashamed

As we've said before, behaviors that allow you to avoid your deep down feelings of shame may help you deal with self-worth problems temporarily, but in the long run do not get rid of shame. Nobody can learn to benefit from shame by ignoring it. Defenses that avoid shame are survival behaviors only; very shamed teens must learn and experience that they are valuable people who are worth love and respect. The way out of shame is: *To Come Out Of Hiding!*

Arrogance

Another defense against feeling bad about yourself is when you convince yourself that you are better than everyone else. There are two ways of showing the attitude that is called "arrogance": (1) Acting like you think that you are better than everyone else or (2) Putting other people down all the time.

Here's an example of type (1): At dance class, Lisa always brags about how she would have done that step "much better than anyone else." She actually is one of the better dancers in the class, but she constantly acts and talks like she's *always* far better than *any* other class member or any other dancer *ever*.

An example of type (2): Wherever Dan goes, he's always putting other people down. It doesn't matter who it is: teachers, friends, kids he notices on the street, TV characters, etc. If he's there, he's got a negative comment about someone. Such as, "Mrs. Smith is ugly," "Chris is stupid," "Mike walks funny;" always a put-down. If you really pay attention, you'll see that Dan never has anything good to say about anyone, except maybe himself.

Some really shamed teens practice acting like they're the greatest; others practice put-downs. Many use both kinds of behavior to protect themselves against their deep down feelings of shame. An arrogant teen places himself on a pedestal where nobody can see his shame; not even he knows how bad he feels inside. The price he pays is not being close to anyone or having real friends. The arrogant person has set himself apart from anyone who wants to befriend or like him. He or she is truly all alone in the world.

Can you think of anyone who uses arrogance as a defense? Is there a part of you that can be that way? How did you learn it?

Exhibitionism

The last survival strategy we'll talk about is showing off, or exhibitionism. This seems to be a really strange reaction because the teenwho is feeling bad about him or herself, instead of hiding, calls attention to him or herself. "Go ahead, look at me if you want," the show-off seems to say, "I've got nothing to hide!" This person may act silly, wild, weird or strange in their dress or behavior.

The show-off insists that we look at what they would really like to hide. For example, some teens who feel strange and different from other people on the inside will wear the most bizarre, shocking or just strange-looking clothes, or dress in an extremely sexy way. Even though they could make much more effort to look attractive or appropriate, they seem to want others to be afraid, put off or avoid them. It's like they are sending out a message saying "look at how terrible, weird or extreme I am." They have survived their shame about their sense of difference by changing their embarrassment into show-off behavior.

Showing off is a really harmful way to avoid feeling shame. Every time the show-off acts the way he does, he sets himself further apart from other people who are annoyed or shocked by his behavior. Threat only makes his shame greater, which he hides by showing off all the more. In a vicious cycle, the show-off finally ends up alone, the object of pity and even more ashamed.

Can you think of anyone who uses exhibitionism as a way to avoid feeling shame? Is there a part of you that can use this defense? How did you learn it?

Review Homework from Last Session

What did you do with the *Broken Record Technique* this past week? Did you have a problem answering the nine questions under *Confronting My Fears About Self-Esteem Behavior* for certain problems and goals? You will be returning to these nine questions as you work on your specific assertiveness problems and goals in later sessions.

Criticism as a Form of Manipulation

Many teens have difficulty dealing with criticism because they experience it as a personal rejection. As a child, you faced criticism from a one-down position. When you made a mistake, older people passed judgment on you: "Carlos, you shouldn't have broken your sister's toy. Bad boy." You were wrong, therefore you were bad (whether you actually meant to break it or not). Eventually, you learned to feel ashamed whenever you were criticized. This is a powerful form of manipulation used to teach children to conform (or behave in a certain way). Less damaging ways of teaching children how to behave include: (1) reinforcing appropriate behavior and ignoring unwanted behavior, (2) pointing out what was wrong with that behavior and suggesting a more desirable alternative behavior, and (3) modeling appropriate behavior.

You probably developed special strategies to minimize the pain of criticism that followed you into adolescence, such as blowing up (and marching away), recalling the faults of the critic or pretending you didn't hear the criticism and yet still feel miserable inside. These aggressive and passive strategies for dealing with criticism can damage your relationships and your self-esteem. Over the course of this Workbook, you will learn seven assertive strategies for dealing with criticism, which will help you keep your relationships and self-esteem intact. These strategies include *acknowledgement, clouding, probing, the content-to-process shift, time-out, slowing down* and *the broken record technique* (which you already learned in Session Two).

Acknowledgement

When someone offers constructive criticism (criticism that is meant to help you, not just point out your errors), you can use this feedback to improve yourself. When you have made a mistake, having someone point it out to you can be helpful in preventing future mistakes.

Whenever you get a criticism with which you agree, whether it is constructive or just a reminder, acknowledge that the critic is right (not an easy thing to do, but try it). For example, "Yes, I did forget to bring my textbook to class. Thanks for reminding me." "You're right, I am late for practice today." "Thanks for letting me know that my voice is too soft for you to hear in the back of the classroom."

You do not need to give excuses or apologies for your behavior. When you were a child, you were asked such questions as "Why did you spill the milk?" or "Why were you ten minutes late?" and you were expected to give reasonable answers. As an adolescent, you can choose to give an explanation for your behavior, but you do not need to. Ask yourself if you really want to, or if you're reacting out of habit.

Clouding

Non-constructive, manipulative criticism (criticism meant to control and direct your behavior) with which you disagree deserves the assertive technique known as clouding. The manipulative critic takes a grain of truth and elaborates on it, using his or her imagination to put you down. For example: "Late with your paper again, Todd? You're always late. I can't imagine how you pass a single class with your terrible work habits. What if everybody in this school were as slow and lazy as you? We'd have to hang a hammock in every classroom!"

Manipulative critics are expert at name-calling and *you*-messages. They bring up old history. They use absolutes such as *always*, *never*, and *everyone*. If you are foolish enough to try to reason with them, you only give them more ammunition for their case. They are not really interested in listening to you, even when they ask you a question. Their secretly low self-esteem forces them to prove that they are right and to always win their point (even if they can actually be nice people when they're not feeling angry and threatened). When you're tempted to try to prove yourself or retaliate in kind to manipulative criticism, try to remind yourself that you will only encourage a senseless argument that you cannot possibly win. If you're still not convinced of this, think back to a time you may have tried to reason or get even with a manipulative critic. Why continue to waste your time doing something so frustrating and unproductive? Instead, you can learn how to stop manipulative critics in their tracks.

Three Ways to Diffuse (Take the Power out of) Manipulative Criticism

Agree in Part

The first way to diffuse criticism is to find some part of the manipulative critic's statement that you think is true, and agree with it (again, a very hard thing to do when someone is criticizing you but easier if you keep your mind on these suggestions). Change the critic's sentence so that you can honestly agree with it. Drop the *absolutes*. And ignore the rest of the message. So, as a response to the example given above, you might simply say, "You're right, I am late with my paper." The critic will usually try to force you into admitting more wrongdoing. But if you continue to find some part of the critic's statements to agree with, she will soon become tired of trying to prove that she is right and you are wrong. After all, it's not much of a challenge to argue with someone who keeps agreeing with you. The secret is not to let yourself become ashamed of her accusation and start defending yourself.

Agree in Probability

A second form of *clouding* which you can use with a manipulative critic is to *Agree in Probability*. Here, you need to find something in what the manipulative critic is saying with which you can probably agree. You can think to yourself that the odds of his or her being right are one in a hundred as you reply, "You're probably right that I'm often late." Again, change the critic's wording slightly so that you don't have to compromise your self-esteem and agree with something you really don't believe.

Agree in Principle

The third and final form of *clouding* is about agreeing with your critic only in principle. This requires a very simple kind of logic, such as if X were true, then Y would also be true. For example, if the teacher said she can't imagine how Todd can pass a single class with her terrible work habits, Todd might respond with "You're right, if I have bad work habits, I *won't* pass my classes."

Homework

Continue practicing the *Broken Record Technique*.

Begin practicing acknowledgement and clouding when you're criticized. Review your experience afterwards, and ask yourself, "What did I say that worked well? How can I improve on my response next time?" Since this kind of thing might not happen too frequently, listen to criticism you might hear directed toward someone else, and imagine how you would respond with acknowledgement or clouding. You can even do this when listening to criticism on TV shows. Take ten minutes to imagine past instances of being criticized, or times that are likely to occur in the future. Imagine successfully using *acknowledgement* or *clouding*.

SESSION FIVE

Healing The Shame: Understanding

Patience – Feeling Better is a Process
(It Happens Over Time)

Becoming Very Aware of Your Shame

Notice the Defenses You Use Against Shame
(Ways You Hide from Shame)

Notice the Reasons for Your Shame

Accept Your Shame as Part of Being Human

Review Homework

Probing

Content-to-Process Shift

Time-Out

Slowing Down

Homework

Healing The Shame: Understanding

 *This time, Rosa caught herself before much damage was done. She usually makes up an excuse and runs away as soon as she starts to feel any bad feelings about herself. Sometimes she leaves without knowing what is bothering her and only later connects it with shame. But today she noticed right away that she was overreacting to one small put-down. Then she could remind herself not to run away. She didn't let that one criticism be turned into a total feeling of "You're just no good" in her mind.*

"I'm finally learning to appreciate my shame. I used to be terrified of it. Now I can sit quietly with my bad feelings some of the time. I try to listen to what my shame tells me about myself, about how I really want to live my life. The most important thing I've recognized is that shame is a part of me. If I hate my bad feelings, I'm actually hating a part of myself."

Bad feelings about yourself drive down your head and eyes. Shame steals energy, hopefulness and excitement. Still, the teen whose face flushes with shame is also someone who wants and needs to learn how to hold his or her head up in calmness and pride. That is the message of hope that lies hidden in every moment of shame.

Patience – Feeling Better is a Process (It Happens Over Time)

Shame is about a person's feelings as a human being. Since the pain and hurt from being shamed is often deep and long lasting, it will take time to feel better. The recovery from shame is a slow process, not a one-time event. You might feel terrible one day, better the next, and maybe awful again on the third.

Being impatient is a big problem as you deal with shame. Naturally, you want to get over that feeling as quickly as possible. But just reading and thinking about shame can sometimes make the problem feel worse than ever. Above all, you need your bad feelings about yourself to just go away so you can feel that it's okay to be in the world.

At first there may be more bad days than good. But after awhile, maybe a few months, or even longer, you may discover that you respect and appreciate yourself much more than when you first began this hard work.

The gift of love to yourself is the payoff for dealing with shame and self-hatred.

Becoming Very Aware of Your Shame

Just how do you become aware of and then start to get over those bad feelings about yourself – the feelings we are calling "shame?" Completing this Workbook and following the exercises and homework assignments is the best start.

Also, try to notice the messages your body gives you. Clues that shame is the problem are blushing, looking down, and sudden loss of energy (that "sinking" feeling). You should also listen carefully to your thoughts, especially the automatic put-downs you give yourself. Likewise, you can see shame in your actions. If you avoid other kids (or adults) at times or get really quiet or shy, you may be feeling shame. Sometimes you might feel like you don't know what to do or get very self-conscious (as if your every move is being watched), especially around critical people.

Notice the Defenses You Use Against Shame
(Ways You Hide From Shame)

Earlier, you learned that very shamed teens often find behaviors and thoughts that make them less aware of their shame (they hide from the shame they feel.) These defenses make the immediate pain of feeling shame less strong, but at the cost of ignoring what is really happening. Think about the common defenses against shame that you may be using:

Denial –pretending that the parts of life that bring us shame don't exist, forcing our real problems out of our minds.

Rage – driving others away with harsh and angry behavior so they cannot see what's wrong with us (our defects). This is most likely to happen if we believe others are trying to make us feel terrible on purpose.

Perfectionism – attempting to get rid of shame by not allowing ourselves to make a mistake.

Arrogance – acting like we're better than everyone or finding fault with everyone else, even strangers. *Exhibitionism*– acting very open and public with behavior that most people would prefer to hide. For example, if we cannot read well, we might call special attention to it in a showy way to convince ourselves and others that it doesn't really bother us.

The goal here is to understand how you protect yourself from painful shame feelings and thoughts, not just to get rid of your defenses. In time, you will be able to make choices about how to defend yourself against bad feelings. For example, if you almost always go away from others when you start to feel shame (or just think someone else might put you down), you should not feel you have to stay around and handle all your shameful feelings in public. Remember, you have the choice to stay or leave, depending on what you feel you can manage at the moment.

Notice the Reasons for Your Shame

It is valuable to sort through the reasons for your bad feelings about yourself because each leads to different plans for getting healthier. For example, if your main problems with shame come from hanging around with a friend who tends to bully you or put you down, you will need a different plan than if most of your feelings of shame come from the kind of family you are in. Many kids discover that their bad feelings about themselves come from several sources.

Accept Your Shame as a Part of Being Human

The understanding stage of getting over shame ends when you accept yourself as a human being that sometimes might feel ashamed. Your shame will not go away by your fearing, hating and fighting it. In fact, it could even grow stronger if you fight it. A teen who hates his shame forgets that he is really just hating a part of himself.

You must accept your shame before you can change it. Shame is what's real! Shame cannot simply be wished away because it is painful. Nor can it be willed away by being tough. It is far better to be a friend to your shame than to treat it with fear or hatred. All of us feel ashamed of ourselves sometimes. Try to make peace with that shame if at all possible, because it really is just another part of you. Kids and teens have to respect every part of themselves, including the bad feelings they have about who they are, in order to discover how to love themselves.

Review Homework

How did you handle criticism this week? What technique did you use? Review how to use *clouding* and *acknowledgement.*

Probing

Sometimes the critic's goals will be unclear. Is the critic trying to help you and simply going about it in an uncool way? Is he or she actually trying to bully or control you while pretending to be helpful? Are the critic's words actually hiding beliefs, feelings and wants that are unspoken? Especially if this critic is someone who matters to you, you may want to find out more about the criticism. This requires listening carefully – a very hard thing to do while being criticized!

Example of Probing

Critic: Late again, I see. One of these days you'll get to the party and find that we've all gone home already.

You: I'm sorry I'm late, but what is there about my being late that bothers you so much?

Critic: You've been getting away with coming and going on your own schedule and I don't like that!

You: What is there about my coming and going on my own schedule that makes you so upset?

Critic: I always break my back to get places on time and lots of times, I have to stop what I'm doing right in the middle. You just march in here whenever you feel like it. Like you're someone special. It's not fair!

You: What do you mean by "not fair?"

Critic: Well, I guess what's not fair about it is that you're *never* on time, while I *always* am –and that's just how I think others expect me to be. But to be honest, maybe how I see things isn't so right.

In this example, probing the critic was useful for placing responsibility for the problem where it really belonged – with the critic instead of you. Often, the critic won't budge from his righteous position and isn't willing to respond to your questions. When you've convinced yourself that the critic is trying to manipulate you, shift from *probing* to *clouding*. If you actually agree with anything the critic says, be sure to *acknowledge* that part.

Be careful when you probe that you do not either verbally or non-verbally give the message: "So what's bugging you now?" (that is, act sarcastic or act like the other person is a nag). If done the right way (and that will take practice), *probing* can turn a manipulative critic into an assertive person who can directly express his or her thoughts, feelings and wishes while also respecting yours.

Content-to-Process Shift

When your conversation with someone gets stuck because of strong feelings or because of different needs or wants, shift the focus of the discussion from that topic to a discussion of what's going on between the two of you.

For example, you assertively ask your best friend to hang out with you more often, and she reacts with: "You feel like I'm ignoring you? Well, I remember last month when you were in the school play, you hardly spoke to me." Rather than getting into an argument about the past, you reply: "We're getting side-tracked into talking about old issues," or "You seem to be angry with me."

Typical problems that you may have in practicing *content-to-process* shift for the first time include:

1. Getting into an explanation of why the other person has gotten off the track, when the purpose of this tool is simply to point out that the conversation has gotten shifted, so that it can be brought back on track again.

Example: You say, "You know, I was trying really hard to impress the drama teacher because I want to be an actress, and I didn't want to get in trouble for slacking off." Friend: "Nice way to treat your best friend!" Here, you could get sidetracked into a discussion about being a good friend

2. Being accused of "analyzing" the other person as an excuse by them to take control of the conversation and manipulate you into feeling wrong. A good response to this is, "I'm just giving you my opinion," and then get right back to the original topic.

Example: Friend: "Why are you always trying to figure out why I'm angry with you? Stop trying to analyze me!"

3. Being told that your comment is wrong, and then getting into an argument about that. Rather than let that happen, use *acknowledgement* or *clouding*, then return to the original topic.

Example: Friend: "I'm not angry with you because you did better on the test. I just always feel angry when I have to take a math test." You: "Yes, I can tell that taking that math test made you feel angry!"

4. Getting completely stuck on the original topic when the *content-to-process shift* comment has brought up something that *ought to* be discussed before going back to the original topic. This happens when the other person has feelings that are so strong that it completely prevents him or her from being able to recognize yours.

Example of Content-to-Process Shift

Naomi: (babysitting): Okay, now that you've watched your favorite TV show, you have to go to bed.

Child: Come on, just one more show. It's a special and it's only half an hour long.

Naomi: No, you have to go to bed now. (This is *the broken record statement*).

Child: You let Anna stay up for special programs; you're being unfair to me.

Naomi: You're getting off the track by bringing up your sister. You have to go to bed now. (*content-to-process shift* and *broken record technique*).

Child: You always treat her better than me. You never give me a break. You're always against me. I hate you!

Naomi: I understand that you're very angry with me, but you still have to go to bed now. (*content-to-process shift* and *broken record technique).*

Child: None of my other sitters would do this to me. My parents will never ask you to sit again when I tell them how mean you've been to me.

Naomi: You're changing the subject again. You have to go to bed now. (*content-to-process* and *broken record technique*).

Child: I remember last time you sat; you let me stay up until midnight watching a movie. There have been lots of times you've let me stay up later. Why not tonight?

Naomi: You're avoiding going to bed by bringing up things that happened in the past. You really have to go to bed now.

Child: You sure are tough.

Time-Out

When you get stuck in a conversation about a topic where there are differences, you may want to postpone the conversation until another time. *Time-Out* is useful when the interaction becomes too passive or too aggressive. One of you may be silent, crying, confused, unready to make a decision or just agreeing with everything the other says (without really meaning it). Or perhaps, you are hitting below the belt by name-calling, bringing up old complaints or being manipulatively critical. If you or the other person feels too pressured to communicate or think at the moment (or if you are tempted to give in to the other's requests without feeling right about it), give yourself time to cool off, reflect on what has been said and return later with the positive intention of communicating instead of merely proving your point and winning. For example, in response to your friend, who is pouting, you assertively call a *time-out*: "This is not a good time to resolve our differences of opinion. Let's talk about it tomorrow." In a situation where you are dealing with an authority (a coach, teacher, parent, etc.), it's not always so easy to assert your right to a *time-out* while there is pressure from the other for you to agree with them immediately. But remind yourself that you have the right to feel comfortable about a situation, even if someone else is expecting you to behave, think or feel a different way.

Slowing Down

Even when you aren't calling a *time-out*, don't feel that you have to respond immediately to every situation. You don't have to produce an instant answer, even if adults are pressuring you to respond. Momentary delays allow you to:

1. Be sure that you understand what the speaker has said.

2. Process (go over in your mind and really understand) what has been said.

3. Become aware of what you think, feel and want in regard to what has been said.

4. Avoid saying things that you may regret later.

5. Consciously influence the situation toward the outcome that you want.

Typical statements that you can use to slow down an interaction include:

1. "This is too important to race through...let's slow it down."

2. "That's an interesting point...let me think about it for a moment."

3. "Wait a minute. I want to give you an honest answer."

4. "Is this what I hear you saying?" (Then repeat what you think you heard while taking time to take it in and reflect on it.)

5. "I'm not sure I understand...could you say that again?"

Homework

You have now learned seven assertive skills for dealing with people who are manipulative or uncooperative: *The Broken Record Technique, Acknowledgement, Clouding, Probing, Content-to-Process Shift, Time-Out* and *Slowing Down.* You must practice these skills so that you will remember to use them instead of falling back into the old habits of being manipulated. You can do this in your imagination, by writing out a script or role-playing alone or with a partner. After every real interaction with a manipulative or uncooperative person, go over your responses in your head. In what ways were you effective in dealing with the manipulation? How might you improve your performance next time? Remember to give yourself credit for any improvement and build on it.

SESSION SIX

Healing The Shame - Taking Action

Get Help – You Don't Have To Do This Alone

Challenge The Shame

Setting Goals Based on Principles

The Principle of Humanity

The Principle of Humility

The Principle of Autonomy

The Principle of Competence

Take Mental And Physical Action To Reach These Goals

Self-Esteem Position Statement

Four Parts of a Self-Esteem Position Statement

Self-Esteem Listening

Self-Esteem Position Statement – Expressing and Listening

Workable Compromise

Homework

Healing The Shame - Taking Action

"All I want to do is feel like a human being. Why is that so hard? What can I do to feel like I belong? Every time I'm around people I just want to run away. I'm so afraid of rejection that I want to stay home all day."

Carlos dreams of being a more independent person. But he doesn't know exactly what independence means. Would he have to do everything on his own? Could he ever ask for help? He has spent so much time pleasing others that he is no longer sure about who he is or what he believes in. He feels ashamed every time he depends on others, but he also feels too weak to stand up on his own.

"I'm tired of failing. I'm tired of expecting that I will mess up anything I touch. How can anyone feel proud when they believe they can't do anything right? I've got to start really trying to do things well."

Feeling bad about yourself (feeling shame) is a messenger, telling you that there is something wrong in your life that you must change. You need to pay attention to that message and take action to help you live a better and more successful and happy life.

Let's look at the five steps to help change painful shame into good behaviors. These five steps have to do with setting positive goals, rather than just trying to get rid of shame.

1. Get help – you don't have to do this alone.
2. Talk back to your shame. Challenge it.
3. Set positive goals based on humanity, humility, autonomy and competence (we're going to explain what this means later in this session.)
4. Take mental and physical action to move toward these goals.
5. Look back at your progress regularly.

Get Help – You Don't Have to Do this Alone

Choosing to be alone is a common reaction to feelings of shame. The more deeply a teen is shamed, the more she will tend to hide her thoughts, feelings and actions from others. A person who is shamed keeps whole areas of her life a secret because she believes that others would put her down if they knew who she really was. Unfortunately, shame grows in secrecy. By hiding who she really is, a teen that feels bad about herself only makes herself more certain that she really is no good.

But the truth is that much of shame grows through our relationships with other teens and adults. This shame can best be helped when we come out of hiding and talk with others. Damage from being shamed begins to go away when this shame is shown to others in a safe way.

Not every teen or adult can be trusted with your bad feelings. Above all, a trusted person is one who will not add to your shame or feelings of badness when he or she is given private information about you. Because you may have difficulty talking about yourself, you need to try to reach out to others at the very times when you feel least good about yourself. You need to move toward others even if you are scared of rejection. At the same time, you need to protect yourself by finding non-shaming people with whom to share, so your attempts at bravery will not be met with cruel attacks on you. (But remember: nobody can react to you in a kind and caring way every single time.)

Talk Back to the Shame – Challenge It

Each kind of shame must be talked to a little differently. For example, a very sad and depressed teen might need to tell herself all five of the following statements at some time while she is getting over her terribly bad feelings about herself:

- "That's my sadness telling me I'm no good. I can't stop that from happening now, but I know it's not true."

- "My Dad tells me I'm worthless and I guess I really used to believe him. But now that I'm getting older and more mature, I don't have to accept those messages any longer. I think I'll give back that shame because it really doesn't belong to me."

75

Or:

- "My Mom seems so ashamed of herself in every way. She can be controlling and critical of my brothers and me, but never asserts herself outside the home. I want to make a special effort not to behave like her, even though I love her."

- "My 'best' friend puts me down ten times a day. It's time for me to tell him clearly that I won't keep listening to him. I'm worth more than that! And if he doesn't stop, I'll walk away (and maybe find a new friend who treats me better)."

- " I'm tired of hating myself. For one thing, I'm going to make myself a promise not to call myself terrible names anymore. I need to treat myself with respect!"

Setting Goals Based On Principles

Four principles are especially important in learning to handle your shame:

- *The Principle of Humanity*

   Everyone belongs to the human race. There are no exceptions. There are no tests to pass, no jobs to do, no possible way to be left out. All people (babies, kids, teens and adults) are human beings, and no amount of shame can take that away.

- *The Principle of Autonomy*

   Each of us (when we are old enough) has the right and responsibility to decide how to live our lives. Teens are learning now how to make those decisions about themselves.

- *The Principle of Humility*

   All human beings are equal – no person is better or worse than another.

- *The Principle of Competence*

   Every person (babies, kids, teens and adults) is good enough to give some value to the world.

Example of a Good Goal Statement: *"I will tell myself that I want to develop the habit of doing well (being competent). I can replace my shame with real pride when I work as hard as I am able. But I also know when to stop. My goal this week is to remind myself on three different days to accept being 'good enough' rather than being perfect."*

Take Mental and Physical Action to Reach These Goals

Shame is a mystery. No simple exercise or plan can possibly cover every part of it. But you can talk back to (challenge) your shame by setting a long-term goal to think and act in ways that move you toward self-respect and feeling better about yourself.

Exercise

First, get four separate sheets of paper and label the top of each sheet with a separate principle: humanity, humility, autonomy and competence. Go back and look over the meaning of each principle. Now, on the left-hand side of the page, write under each heading anything that you think or do that takes you away from this principle (For example, if you sometimes call yourself "a pig" or "a piece of poop," those names would be going against the principle of humanity. You're calling yourself something that's not human.) Then ask yourself what you need to do to change each item, and write down those answers next to the original thought or behavior. Choose one or two things that you could change. Start with ones that are simple and clear. Finally, promise yourself to try and make those changes in your daily life, remembering that shame heals slowly and that you don't have to be perfect.

Review your Homework from Last Session

What did you do with the manipulative or uncooperative people in your life this week? How did you practice your seven *self-esteem skills* to deal with manipulative people?

Self-Esteem Position Statement

When you want to express yourself on a specific topic, use a *Self-Esteem Position Statement.* The topic may be a small one, like what movie you want to go to, or a major one, like telling a bully to treat you with respect. In any case, you need to express your position clearly and completely, because partial communication can lead to misunderstandings and frustration.

Exercise: Fill out the *Self-Esteem Position Statement* below.

Self-Esteem Position Statement

<u>Instructions</u>: Use this form to write self-esteem positions for four situations in your life in which you would like to express your position clearly.

Situation 1: (Describe)_____

I think (your point of view) _____

I feel_____

I want_____

If you_____

Situation 2: (Describe)_____

I think (your point of view) _____

I feel_____

I want_____

If you_____

Situation 3: (Describe)_____

I think (your point of view) _____

I feel_____

I want_____

If you_____

Situation 4: (Describe)_____

I think (your point of view)_____

I feel_____

I want_____

If you_____

Four Parts of a Self-Esteem Statement:

1. Your point of view on the situation

2. Your feelings

3. Your wants

4. A reinforcement to encourage the other person to cooperate

A Self-Esteem Statement contains four parts. The first part is your definition of the problem, or how you see the situation. It's essential for focusing the discussion. Here is your opportunity to share your opinion and beliefs about the issue at hand. Try to be non-blaming (no matter how you really feel inside). Use non-aggressive language that states the problem as objectively as possible. For example: "It's time to make a decision about what movie we're going to see tonight. I know you love action movies, but the last three movies we've seen have been that kind. We really need to try something new."

The second part, your feelings, gives the other person a better understanding of how important an issue is to you. Do not substitute an opinion ("I think all action movies should be closed down!") for a feeling. An example of a feeling is: "I hate action movies."' Once they are expressed, your feelings can often play a major role in helping you get what you want, especially when your opinion differs greatly from that of your listener. If nothing else, the listener may be able to relate to and understand your feelings about an issue, even when he or she totally disagrees with your point of view. When you share your feelings, you become less of an enemy. Expression of your feelings often makes possible either an agreement to disagree or a workable compromise. Unfortunately, feelings are often left out of a communication.

The third part, your wants, is best stated in a simple sentence or two. Instead of expecting others to read your mind and magically meet your needs, as in the case of a *passive* individual, you clearly state your wishes and needs. Try to be specific about what you want. Ask people to change *behaviors*, not attitudes! Rather than assuming that you are always right and entitled to get your way, as an *aggressive* person might, state your wants as *preferences* rather than commands. For example, "I would really *like* to go to a comedy tonight."

The fourth part is to motivate the other person to give you what you want by reinforcing his cooperation. Let the other person know how he will benefit by cooperating with you: "I'll be less grumpy and more fun to be with if we go to the kind of movie I like." "I'll go to an action movie with you next weekend." If the other person is very resistant, positive reinforcement may not work. In such cases, state the negative consequences for failure to cooperate. When stating negative consequences, do not make threats such as this: "If we don't go to a comedy, I don't think we should be friends anymore." This only makes the other person defensive and angry. Instead, say how you will take care of yourself if your wishes are not accommodated: "If you won't agree to go to a comedy, I'll invite Jon to go with me instead since he likes comedies."

Examples of the Self-Esteem Position Statement:

"You've interrupted me three times since I started to tell this story. It makes me feel angry and disrespected. I would appreciate you holding off with your comments until I finish what I'm trying to say. Then I promise to be quiet and listen to what you have to say."

"In talking with you about our science projects, I realize we seem to have a lot in common. It's really been fun getting to know you better. Why don't you come over to my house on Saturday, if you're free, so we can talk more about stuff."

"Mom, I know the rule is that I finish my homework before I can go out with friends, but Lynn invited me over to see her new prom dress. I'm really excited to see what it looks like and she'll be away all weekend. If I promise to be back in half an hour and finish all my work then, I'd like you to make an exception this time. I'll still be able to finish all my homework before bedtime."

Expressing your thoughts, feelings and wants in an assertive position statement improves the chance that the message you want to send will be the same message that the listener hears. Notice that these assertive position statements do not blame or use attacking labels. The listener is unlikely to become highly defensive, tune out what you are saying and prepare a counterattack or run away. The situations are described specifically and objectively without slipping into negative judgments. By using *I-messages* rather than *you-messages* (talking just about what *you* want, feel and need), you own your own opinions, feelings and wants. When you do this you will appear more mature and confident. Also, when delivering an *assertive* position statement, remember to use good posture, direct eye contact and speak in a calm voice (not so easy to put all together, but practice makes it work).

A *Self-Esteem Position Statement* is difficult to ignore or misunderstand. Just in case, check to be sure that your listener is following what you're saying. You can do this by occasionally asking the listener to summarize what he or she heard you say. If their response is accurate, you can safely move ahead. Don't ask your listener, "Do you understand?" (That may sound like you think they're dumb.) Instead you might say, "I'd like to hear what you think I said." Or "Could you say back to me what I've just told you, so I can be sure I'm making myself clear?"

Self-Esteem Listening

When you are listening to a *Self-Esteem Position Statement* , you will focus your attention on the other person so that you can accurately hear the speaker's opinions, feelings and wishes. This is difficult when, at the same time, you are very aware of your own opinions, feelings and wishes (which will be quite different from those of the other person). Use the techniques of *slowing down* and *time-out* when appropriate. Assertive listening involves three steps:

1. **Prepare:** Become aware of your own feelings and needs. Are you ready to listen? Are you sure that the other person is ready to speak?

2. **Listen:** Give your full attention to the other person: listen to the speaker's perspective, feelings and wants. If you are uncertain about one

of these three elements, ask the speaker for more information. *Examples*: "I'm not quite sure how you see the situation…could you say more about it?" "How do *you* feel about this?" "I don't understand what you want…could you be more specific?"

3. **Acknowledge:** Communicate to the other person that you heard his or her view on the subject by using *reflective listening* (mirroring back to the person what you heard him or her to say). *Example*: "I understand that you don't want to help me with my report right now because you feel overwhelmed with studying for your own exam." Another way to acknowledge the other's feelings is to share your own feelings about what has been said: "I'm feeling overwhelmed, too, and I feel really bad about having to ask you to do even more work."

Self-Esteem Position Statement – Expressing and Listening

When you are involved in a heated conflict with another person, the two of you can take turns using assertive expressing and listening. Many problems are resolved simply by stating clearly what each of you thinks, feels and wants. This can often clear up misunderstandings or create unexpected solutions to problems. Opportunities for this type of communication happen often between people who live, work or go to school together. Sometimes these opportunities happen by accident, but often you need to arrange a convenient time and place for the two of you to discuss the problem.

Read the following example:

Carlos: I'd like to talk to you about a problem. Is this a good time?

Bob: Not really. I need to get to my next class early. I should have some free time after that.

Carlos: (after the next class): This may seem like a small thing to you, but it's been bothering me ever since the school year began. I really don't like that you flip my hat off every time you pass me in the hallway. I'm sick and tired of having to put my books down and pick up my hat. And sometimes when I'm rushing, I get to class late because of the extra time that takes. Plus, it's embarrassing.

Bob: Well, I understand why it would bother you to get to class late for something like that and I hear that you're angry. But I do that to all the freshman guys – it's just a way of being friendly. I never thought it was such a big deal.

Carlos: Well, whether it's meant to be friendly or not – I still don't like it.

Bob: I think you're making a big deal over nothing. None of the other freshman guys are complaining. And older guys did it to me when I was a freshman.

Carlos: Yeah, I see you're point. I feel stuck. Even though I may be asking for something you think is unfair, I still want you to stop.

Bob: Look, if you stop making such a big deal about this, I'll try not to do it all the time – maybe just once in a while.

Carlos: Okay – we'll try that, but let's talk again after a few weeks to see if we need another solution. Maybe I don't really want to be friendly with someone who gets me upset!

Bob: I'm game – let's try the easier solution first and see if it works.

Workable Compromise

When two people's interests are in direct conflict, a fair compromise that totally satisfies both sides is very hard, if not impossible, to achieve. Instead, you can look for a workable compromise you can both live with, at least for a while. Here are a few examples of workable compromises:

- *My way when I do it, your way when you do it.*

- *My way this time, your way next time.*

- *Part of what I want and part of what you want.*

- *If you'll do X for me, I'll do Y for you.*

- *We'll try my way this time, and if you don't like it, you don't have to do it next time.*

Although a compromise may naturally come up in your discussion, you sometimes need a *brainstorming* session to come up with one. *Brainstorming* a workable compromise involves the following four steps:

1. Make a list of all the possible solutions you can think of. Let your imaginations run wild while creating as many solutions to the problem as possible. *Don't* judge any of the suggestions at this stage of *brainstorming* (nothing is too silly or dumb for you to consider).

2. Cross off the solutions that are not acceptable to both of you.

3. Decide on a workable compromise that you can both live with.

4. Agree to review your compromise after a specific length of time (say, a month). If you aren't both satisfied enough, you can renegotiate (go over the earlier steps to come up with a new solution). If your compromise seems to have resolved the conflict fairly well, congratulate yourselves!

Another approach to finding a workable compromise involves asking the other person to counter your proposal (come up with their own compromise solution). If you find their counterproposal to be unacceptable, be sure that you understand the feelings and needs of the other person about this issue, then come up with another proposal of your own. Continue back and forth until you come up with a new proposal you can both live with.

Example of a Workable Compromise:

Mom: Okay Lucy, we clearly expressed how we see the problem, how we feel about it and what we want; yet no easy solution has been found that we can both live with. Your Dad and I want you to spend our summer vacation at the shore with the family and you want to spend it here with your friends. Let's *brainstorm* and see if we can come up with some new solutions that might be okay for all of us.

Lucy: That's okay with me. I'll do the writing. Here's one alternative that neither of us has thought of: We can invite all my good friends to the shore with us!

Dad: No way, our house is too small for all your friends. And besides, together you're all too noisy for me!

Mom: No judgments at this point. We just put down whatever comes to mind.

Dad: Okay – sorry. Let's have a family vacation at the beach this year, and Lucy can stay home with her friends next summer. Or we could go to the beach for one week and then all spend the other week here at home.

Lucy: Or you could rent another house at the shore big enough for me and my friends, too.

Mom: Or maybe we could ask one of our neighbors at the shore if they might have some extra room for a couple of your best friends so that they can join us for a weekend.

Dad: Or maybe you wouldn't mind going to the mountains for a couple of weeks with the family. You know the house we rent there is big enough for a few of your friends, too.

Mom: I'm ready to stop *brainstorming* now; I've run out of ideas.

Lucy: Me, too. Let's cross off the ideas that none of us can stand. I refuse to wait until next summer to be with my friends. I feel like a baby spending the whole vacation just with my family.

Dad: And renting another house at the shore is just too expensive for me to do.

Mom: And I don't want to spend a lot of time at home this summer. I need to get away.

Dad: So how does spending a couple of weeks in the mountains sound? You can invite some friends there and Mom will get out of town.

Lucy: That's not my first choice, but I guess it could work out okay. I'd also be willing to spend some time at the shore with just you and Mom, if next year you let me stay home.

Mom: That sounds fine to me.

Dad: It's a deal!

Homework

Practice *Self-Esteem Position Statements, Self-Esteem Listening* and *Workable Compromise* in your imagination, and in real life. Next week, you'll practice putting these three skills together in different problem situations.

SESSION SEVEN

Healing the Shame From Your Family

Don't Get Stuck in the Past

Finding the "You're No Good" Messages from Your Family

Let Yourself Feel Sad About What These Messages Stole From You

Working on Self-Esteem Problems and Goals

Exercise: Self-Esteem Problems and Goals Practice

Homework

Healing The Shame From Your Family

"My Mom kept telling me that I was lazy and stupid. She told me I wasn't good for anything. But now that I'm a teen, I don't need to believe that stuff any longer. I can still hear her saying those things to me, but now I refuse to accept it. Just because she gave me a coat of shame doesn't mean I have to keep wearing it forever."

Carlo's Dad is a functioning alcoholic (a person who can't control his drinking, but who goes to work, has some friends and seems to manage). Even as a very young child, Carlos knew something wasn't normal about his family,. His ears burn with shame when he sees his mother and father argue. Funny that his father never seems to notice and just keeps on embarrassing the whole family. For years now, Carlos has been carrying the family shame with him wherever he goes. He feels his *Dad's* shame, and he needs to give it back.

"My parents argued all the time when I was growing up. My sister and I used to hide in the bedroom and turn the TV up real loud to drown out the noises. Then they got divorced and things got quieter. But my Dad got married again really soon. Now he has another family and I hardly get to see him anymore. It makes me feel so bad that sometimes I don't want to go to school or see anybody. I know it's not me – it's him who ought to be ashamed of not being a better Dad. One of these days, I'm going to find the courage to tell him just that."

 Lucy's Dad seemed to work all the time when she was little. He barely had the time to kiss her good night when he came home from work. He never got to more than a couple of her recitals or softball games all through her elementary and middle school years. Now that she's a teen she feels like he's a complete stranger and that she was never good enough for him to be the way she wanted. As a teen, Lucy needs to understand that her *Dad* didn't understand what it meant to be a good father and that she never did anything wrong.

"My parents are really terrific people. They never argued when I was growing up. They both tried to be involved in all my school activities and sports events. We always went on great family vacations and my friends always want to be around them. The problem is that neither one of them

seems to be able to stand up to anybody. My father always helps every neighbor who asks him and my mom is nice to everyone, even if they don't deserve it. I'm beginning to see why it's so hard for me to stand up for my rights. I'm turning out to be just like them, but I wish I could learn to be different."

"I always thought of my parents as good people. My father was always around, always in charge and very much "the family man." And my mother seemed loving and caring and supportive. It wasn't until I got a lot older that I started to realize that it never really felt okay to ask for anything for myself. My father would get tense and angry and my mother would just "forget" that I had asked, or they would both accuse me of 'selfishness'. But mostly, they both just seemed overwhelmed by the responsibility of being parents. All of us kids learned before we were teens just never to ask. I've really worked hard to teach myself that being "selfish"(thinking about yourself) is sometimes the only right way to be, if you want to have healthy self-esteem."

It is as if you carry around with you a set of parents who live inside your head. These "parental images" might remind you again and again that you are no good or that it's not nice to assert yourself. These parental images may remain as they are even after you grow up and both you and your parents really change a lot. They may still remain even if your parents no longer shame you as they once did, or your parents no longer act as unassertively as they used to. The most common kinds of behavior that causes shame from the family are:

- Messages that you are not good, not good enough, not lovable, too bold, too selfish or that you do not belong or shouldn't exist

- Threats of leaving, neglect, no interest in you or who you are

- Physical and sexual abuse

- Keeping secrets

- Parents who insist that either they or you must be perfect

Don't Get Stuck in the Past

The idea of looking at your past is to discover how the actions of others have hurt you, so that you can change the thoughts, feelings and behaviors that you have now. While you are exploring the causes of your shame, you will feel bad. But it is important that you get through the pain rather than get stuck in it. You must bring your head as well as your heart with you, so you can try to understand how things really and truly are.

Try not to exaggerate as you explore the past. Probably no parents *always* shamed his or her kids. See if you can recall some times when your parents or other family members praised you, helped you and clearly appreciated you. Remember that you are dealing with people, not monsters.

The more deeply you have been shamed, the harder it will be to unglue yourself from past disappointments, sadness, pain and rejections. As you explore the cave of your past, let your friend, a kind parent or other adult be your rope, and let your promise of your own better health be your flashlight.

Finding the "You're No Good" Messages You Got From Your Family

The most important "you're no good" messages are those that affected you the most deeply. These messages might feel right when you say them to yourself: "Yes, my Dad always called me a dummy. But he was right. I do act kind of stupid." The messages are painful, and they seem fixed forever. Write down three important "you're no good" messages (For example: "Try not to eat like a pig" or "Don't be rude to other kids."):

1.

2.

3.

It is helpful if you can remember real times when you were younger (or right now) when you've gotten "you're no good" messages. Maybe you were called clumsy or lazy by a parent as you did chores. Maybe a parent no longer touched you (in a caring way) as you got older, or a parent or other authority figure touched you in a way that made you feel uncomfortable. Maybe a parent gets embarrassed when you say how you feel or what you want. The times you remember may be powerful or small, happening regularly, just sometimes or only once.

Let Yourself Feel Sad About What These Messages Stole From You

"You're bad" or "you're no good" messages and other shaming behaviors deeply affect the young child. A kid who got or is getting these kinds of messages will have many needs that don't get met. As that kid becomes a teen he or she must feel sad about those unmet needs.

Here are a few examples of "you're no good" messages:

- not good

- not good enough

- don't belong

- are not lovable

- should not be or be here

- are too rough, too big, too small

- are selfish

All kids want to hear that they are loved, that they belong, that they are good enough just the way they are and that they are totally acceptable to their family. They need to be assured that they are human, normal and capable. These reasonable needs are not met in families that constantly shame their kids.

Some things that you lose can never be replaced. No amount of praise or respect later in life can make up for the lack of praise or respect received as a kid. That is why feeling very sad or unhappy (what we call "in mourning") is a necessary part of healing shame. You must "mourn" the parts of you that seemed to die as you experienced rejection.

When we can face the sadness resulting from shame, it may feel like a terrible, deep sorrow that can fill us with pain. But this kind of feeling can do away with shame when we let ourselves feel it as much as possible. It helps us to put away the past, with its lost hopes, so we can find a new path to the future.

Review your Homework from Last Session

What did you do with *the Self-Esteem Position Statements, Self-Esteem Listening* and *Workable Compromise*? Briefly review these three skills.

Working on Self-Esteem Problems and Goals

Self-Esteem Problems and Goals

Instructions: Rate situations on a 1 to 4 scale in terms of their *importance* and the *difficulty* in achieving *assertive* behavior:

Four Social Situations in Which I Have Self-Esteem Problems	*Importance*	*Difficulty*	*Total*

Examples:

1. *Problem*:

   Goal: _____ X _____ = _____

2. *Problem*:

   Goal: _____ X _____ = _____

3. *Problem*:

   Goal: _____ X _____ = _____

4. Problem:

Goal: _____ X _____ = _____

                                                          Total   _____

Exercise: – Self-Esteem Problems and Goals Practice

Review your *Self-Esteem Problems and Goals* list. You probably have at least a couple of problems or goals that you have not practiced yet. Go over these in your mind, and imagine *role-playing* them, using the skills you've learned.

If you have any fears or concerns about being assertive in a particular situation, ask the nine questions under *Confronting Your Fears About Being Assertive* section. Remind yourself of your *assertive rights* whenever you need to. Ask yourself what *assertive skills* you imagine yourself using.

Homework: *Practicing New Self-Esteem Skills*

Continue practicing new *Self-Esteem Skills*. Practice applying *Self-Esteem Techniques* to specific problem situations in your imagination, in *role-plays* and then, in real life.

SESSION EIGHT

More Healing the Shame From Your Family: Challenge Old "Put-Down" Messages and Replace with Positive Ones

Challenge Your Behavior So It Supports Self-Worth

Challenge Exercise

Return "Borrowed Shame"

Think About Forgiving So You Can Let Go of Your Shame

Express Negative Emotion– Saying "No"

Review *Self-Esteem Problems and Goals*

A New Beginning

Evaluation

More Healing the Shame From Your Family: Challenge Old "Put-Down" Messages and Replace with Positive Ones

The best thing that can happen to you if you come from a shaming family is to get older. No matter how terrible your situation, you are not as helpless as you were when you were a little kid. As an older kid or teen, you can challenge the bad messages you got as a child. You may have had almost no choice about accepting those messages before, but you can replace them now with much healthier ones.

Remember, those messages started outside of you. They may have been sitting inside your head for a long time now, but they did not begin there. You can sort through the messages you got as a small kid and actually decide to throw some of them out. When you challenge the put-down messages you got as a young kid, you should take the following steps:

- First, make sure you remember, as exactly as possible, each shaming message you got.

- Second, make sure you remember the person or persons who sent each message.

- Third, question the idea that the message *must* be true.

- Fourth, think hard about that message and accept it or reject it.

- Fifth, find new, positive non-shaming messages instead of the old put-downs.

Challenge Exercise

1. Write down 3 – 5 shaming messages (for example, "you're stupid" or "you're spoiled").

2. Write down the names of the person or persons who sent each message.

3.   Question the idea that each message must be true.

4.   Think about each message and accept or reject it.

5.   Find new, positive non-shaming messages to substitute for the old put-downs (*For example, "When I don't understand something, I work very hard to figure it out" instead of "I'm stupid;" "I have high standards" instead of "I'm spoiled"*).

Challenge Your Behavior So It Supports Self-Worth

The hard work talked about in the last section pays off when you change your actions to live a healthier, less shamed life. This new behavior may begin with your group of friends and other close relationships. At some point, though, you will have to change your behavior with your family and with other adults who act as "authority figures"(like teachers, coaches and others whose job it is to tell you how to behave).

Shame that started in your family heals best when you change the way you are *with* your family. Parents *do not* have the right to shame their children just because they are parents. "Dad," you might say, "you called me an airhead for a long time. I'm not an airhead and I've never been one. Please don't call me that again."

These "confrontations" (what we call questioning other people directly) will not be easy. They will probably be reacted to with anger and excuses, especially if the shaming attack was on purpose. The best challenges to a shaming family are those that you can say calmly and clearly. That will be hard for you to do. They may also have to be repeated over and over, because shaming families tend to return to old shaming behaviors out of habit.

Some family members or other authority figures *can* change, and some do so fairly quickly once they learn that you insist on fair treatment. Others will change more slowly or not at all. You will have to decide how much time and energy you are willing to spend in changing your family's behaviors.

Return "Borrowed Shame"

Shame is "catching" in shaming families. It can easily pass from one family member to another, finally infecting everyone. Sometimes one or more family members (often kids or teens) will gather the shame that really belongs to another family member. The shame is transferred from its rightful owner to a more helpless, smaller family member.

This shame is called "borrowed" to keep the idea that it can be returned to its original owner. The idea is that, at one time, a family member was "loaned" shame against his or her will (they didn't know it didn't belong to them). This shame started from the behavior or ideas of another, usually more powerful, family member (like a parent). Now, *that* shame must be returned so the less powerful person (such as a kid or teen) can own a non-shaming view of himself. What is meant by returning "borrowed shame" is letting others be responsible for their own behavior or feelings and admit that those feelings really belong to them.

Borrowed shame may be given to a certain family member either on purpose or by chance. Often, it happens when the family cannot stand the bad feelings about the real problem. For example, it is far easier (but not at all fair or right) to blame and shame a child than to admit to a father's drunkenness. (*"You ought to be ashamed of yourself, young lady. If you were better behaved and caused less unhappiness around here, your father wouldn't get so upset and have to drink."*)

Certain kids may be blamed the most for family troubles. But others in the family may also "borrow" shame. Other kids are held up as examples and feel guilt and shame when they fail to keep everybody happy and everything perfect. Parents actually can and do sometimes feel "borrowed shame" for the actions of their child, too.

The key to getting rid of shame that is actually "borrowed shame" is to notice when you are feeling shame about something that has nothing really to do with your actions, but comes from another family member's or friend's behavior. If you are returning "borrowed shame," you may tell yourself:

"Long ago I took on some shame that didn't belong to me. I thought it was mine at the time. So did the rest of my family. But now I know that I did nothing at the time that was wrong. I'm not guilty, and I have nothing to feel ashamed about."

You can directly tell these thoughts to your family members if you think that some of them can understand what you mean or if family members continue to insist on shaming you. The main goal here is for you to return borrowed shame that makes you feel bad, not to punish others by insisting that they now should feel as bad as you have felt.

Think About Forgiving So You Can Let Go of Your Shame

Forgiveness can hurt a lot. It can bring strong feelings of anger, hatred and deep sadness to the surface. These feelings are the reaction to realizing the terrible damage and destruction that has been caused by being weighed down with so much shame.

Feeling very angry is what *should* happen as you look back at your years as a little kid who has suffered from shaming and put-downs. The anger tells us that something wrong happened. It can give us the energy to help change our thoughts and behaviors. But we should be careful that our anger doesn't turn into resentment (wanting to hurt and punish others for their wrongs), a far less helpful feeling. A resentful kid or teen is someone who is holding on to anger and does not want to give it up and move ahead with his life.

Forgiveness is a way to let go of resentments. The purpose of forgiveness is to help make ourselves healthy. Sometimes, forgiveness can lead to making up with the person who has hurt us and caused us so much pain and unhappiness. Or forgiveness can help us end a relationship that was only about pain and resentment, and get on with our lives.

Remember, forgiveness is by *choice*. Maybe we feel that the pain and sadness are too great to forgive. Maybe we want to forgive but can't find it in our hearts to do so right now. Forgiving only works when we know it is our choice. If we forgive another, we do not have to love them, be their friend or forget about what has happened. Forgiving happens when we can have a thought like this:

99

"I am tired of being resentful and stuck in the past. It only adds to my shame. I am ready to forgive the people who shamed me so that I can get on with my life."

Expressing Negative Feelings – Saying "No"

Learning how to say "no" and express negative feelings is another important skill you need to develop. Self-esteem problems often come from families in which there were poor boundaries and limits. Your parents have probably been either too easy, too strict or inconsistent (sometimes too easy and other times too strict, or always too easy about some things and too strict about others). Also, it may have been unacceptable for you to express negative feelings appropriately (that is, to be *assertive*). As a result, you were never taught the skills needed to maintain appropriate boundaries, set limits with others and express negative feelings.

You probably have already realized that a major trigger is pushed when you feel forced to say or do things that you aren't comfortable with or when you have to act as though you feel something that you don't. You don't feel able or confident about how to <u>not</u> do what is being asked of you. Learning and developing your ability to say "no" confidently can put you back in control of yourself and raise your self-esteem at the same time.

Can you think about some moments in the recent past when you would have loved to say "no?"

Write about one such situation.

You may feel that "what's done is done." But often you *can* go back and "fix" a problem situation by expressing your feelings to the person who was a part of one. No one expects that you'll always express yourself perfectly the first time. Most people are willing to hear you out, even if it's about something that happened quite a while ago. And you can achieve two benefits from doing this. First, you might work out a problem with someone and feel better about him or her and *yourself.* Second, by practicing going back and working out old problems, you will slowly develop the ability to face issues right when they are happening.

Review:

Complete the *Self-Esteem Problems and Goals* form below. Notice the change from the first time you did this form in Session One.

Self-Esteem Problems and Goals

Instructions: rate problems on a 1-to-5 scale based on their *importance* and the *difficulty* in achieving associated assertive behavior goals.

Five Social Situations in which I have difficulty with my assertive behavior:	*Importance*	*Difficulty*	*Total*

Examples:
1. Problem: I always say "yes" to my friends whenever they ask me to do anything (passive).

   Goal: I'd like to say "no" when I don't really feel like doing what they ask.

2. Problem: I never ask my teacher for help (passive).

   Goal: I truly want to ask for help when I can't figure the problem out by myself.

3. Problem: I let older or bigger kids take advantage of me because I don't want to get into a fight (passive).

   Goal: I want to be able to tell them what I want calmly and directly without getting beaten up or embarrassed.

4. Problem: I get tongue-tied when I try to express something positive to my boyfriend/girlfriend, so I don't do it (passive).

   Goal: I want to tell him/her how much I like him/her and how much I appreciate his/her support.

5. Problem: I tend to blow up at my Mom/Dad when they don't want to do things my way (aggressive).

   Goal: I would like to calmly tell them what I want to do and accept having to compromise.

Total   = ____

Falling Back into Old Habits

Replacing *Passive, Passive-Aggressive,* and *Aggressive communication* with *Self-Esteem Communication* requires a lifetime commitment. It's easy to return to old ways of behaving at times when you're under stress, such as when you're tired, hungry, afraid, guilty, ashamed or trying to do too much. As soon as you catch yourself – whether it's just minutes or hours later – go over what happened. Ask yourself what was going on that prevented you from being assertive. Remember that you have a right to make mistakes; learn from them rather than dwell on them.

Review your *Assertive Rights.* Explore your fears to make sure that they're realistic, and ask yourself if it is worth it to you to be assertive in this situation. Focus on the constructive things you said or did, so that the next time that situation comes up you'll be more assertive. Ask yourself what *assertiveness skills* you could use the next time you're in the same or a similar situation. *Role-play* self-esteem communication in the situation in your mind, in front of a mirror, on a tape or with a friend. Include what you think the other person would say. When you anticipate a difficult situation, mentally *role-play* self-esteem communication including the other person's responses.

A New Beginning

 You have finished The Self-Esteem Workbook for Teens. Your thoughts and feelings have been stirred up and you have learned some important *coping skills* and ideas that will serve you well if you continue to work at them. This experience has not been easy and you can take some time right now to congratulate yourself for a job well done! It would be a good idea to review these sessions often because they will take on new value and meaning each time you do.

We hope you have found yourself with fewer feelings of shame, a greater sense of hope and higher self-esteem. Even more, we hope that you will use it to help you create a world where all teens (and all human beings) are accepted without fear. Most of all, we wish you a life that is centered around appreciating and respecting other children, teens and adults. You are now on your way to a new beginning.

Evaluation: Teens

1. What is your overall opinion of this Workbook? *(1 being "worthless," 10 being "extremely helpful")*

1	2	3	4	5	6	7	8	9	10

2. Which session was the most difficult for you? Why?

3. Which session was the most helpful? Why?

4. Did the Workbook meet your expectations? *(1 being "not at all," 10 being "greatly")*

1	2	3	4	5	6	7	8	9	10

Evaluation: Adult Helpers

1. What is your overall opinion of this Workbook? *(1 being "worthless", 10 being "extremely helpful")*

1	2	3	4	5	6	7	8	9	10

2. What do you think about the organization of the Workbook? How would you change it?

3. What suggestions would you make to improve this Workbook?

APPENDIX

Self-Esteem Rights

Self-Esteem Rights are so important for teens to recognize and understand, that some time will be spent reviewing and learning about them in detail.

1   You have a right to put yourself first sometimes

2   You have a right to make mistakes

3   You a right to be the final judge of your feelings and accept them as legitimate

4   You have a right to express your own opinions and beliefs

5   You have a right to change your mind

6   You have a right to question what you don't like and to protest unfair treatment

7   You have a right to interrupt or to ask for clarification

8   You have a right to negotiate for change

9   You have a right to ask for help or emotional support

10   You have a right to feel and express pain or uncomfortable feelings

11   You have a right to ignore advice of others

12   You have a right to receive recognition for your special qualities and talents and for your work and achievements

13   You have a right to say "no" to other people's requests

14   You have a right to be alone, even if others request your company

15   You have a right not to justify yourself to others

16   You have a right not to take responsibility for somebody else's problem

17   You have a right not to have to anticipate the needs and wishes of others

18   You have a right not to worry about the good will of others

19   You have a right to choose not to respond to a question or situation

20   You have a right to say "I don't know" or "I don't understand"

Self Esteem Behavior Log

Date	Behavior	Person	+ Aspects	- Aspects	Aggressive, Passive, Passive-Agg, Assertive

About the Author

ANITA BOHENSKY, Ph.D., is Director/Founder of the Whole Child and Adolescent Center, Clinical Psychologist, Psychotherapist, and Psychoanalyst. She is experienced in helping parents and their pre-school, school age or adolescent children resolve their problems.

Dr. Bohensky works to help children, adolescents and adults with:

- Learning Disabilities/ADD/ADHD
- Difficulties with Divorce and Separation
- Depression
- Anxiety Disorders
- Relationship Issues
- Physical, Emotional, or Sexual Trauma
- Anger Problems

She is a graduate of New York University where she received her Doctor of Philosophy in Developmental Psychology. She has received a Certificate in Psychoanalysis and Psychotherapy from the Postgraduate Center for Mental Health, New York, NY. She also has extensive experience working with, and has been involved in numerous research projects related to, the emotional and social development of children. Dr. Bohensky has been a Consultant in Learning Disabilities/Attention Deficit Disorder/and Childhood Psychopathology at New York Foundling Hospital, Abbott House in Rockland and Westchester Counties, and SUNY Learning Disability Division. This inspired her enthusiastic interest in the learning, anger management, and self-esteem problems of children and adolescents.

Dr. Bohensky has an abiding interest in the psychoanalytic basis of behavior, which underlies her work as Faculty member, Supervisor and Training Analyst at various Psychotherapy Institutes in New Jersey and New York City. Besides her work at the Whole Child / Adolescent Center she is presently a Supervisor and Assistant Adjunct Professor at Columbia University Teachers College, and a Supervisor at Postgraduate Center for Mental Health.

Additional Books from Growth Publishing

Anger Management Workbook for Kids and Teens
ISBN: 1-893505-06-5   Author: Anita Bohensky
Online Description of Anger Management Workbook for Kids and Teens
http://www.growthcentral.com/AngerManagementWorkbook.htm

Real Solution Self Esteem Workbook
ISBN: 1-893505-15-4   Author: Richard Pfeiffer
Online Description of Real Solution Self Esteem Workbook
http://www.growthcentral.com/SelfEsteemWorkbook.htm

Creating Real Relationships – **Overcoming the Power of Difference and Shame**
ISBN: 1-893505-13-8   Author: Richard Pfeiffer
Online Description of Creating Real Relationships
http://www.growthcentral.com/CreatingRealRelationships.htm

Real Solution Anger Management Workbook
ISBN: 1-893505-18-9   Author: Richard Pfeiffer
Online Description of Real Solution Anger Management Workbook
http://www.growthcentral.com/AngerManagementWorkbook.htm

Real Solution Assertiveness Workbook
ISBN: 1-893505-01-4   Author: Richard Pfeiffer
Online Description of Real Solution Assertiveness Workbook
http://www.growthcentral.com/AssertivenessWorkbook.htm

Real Solution Anxiety/Panic Workbook
ISBN: 1-893505-02-2   Author: Richard Pfeiffer
Online Description of Real Solution Anxiety/Panic Workbook
http://www.growthcentral.com/AnxietyPanicWorkbook.htm

Real Solution Binge/Compulsive Eating Workbook
ISBN: 1-893505-17-0   Author: Richard Pfeiffer
Online Description of Real Solution Binge/Compulsive Eating Workbook
http://www.growthcentral.com/BingeEatingWorkbook.htm

Online Resources

Whole Child/Adolescent Center
http://wholechild.net

Growth Central
http://growthcentral.com

AngerHelp.com
http://Angerhelp.com